LBJs Made Easier

Watching Birds in Southern Africa

LBJs
Little Brown Jobs Made Easier

Kenneth Newman **Derek Solomon**
David Johnson **Alex Masterson**

Illustrations by
Kenneth Newman
Penny Meakin

Struik Publishers (Pty) Ltd
(a member of The Struik New Holland
Publishing Group (Pty) Ltd)
Cornelis Struik House
80 McKenzie Street
Cape Town 8001

Reg. No.: 1954/000965/07

First Published by Southern Books (Pty) Ltd 1998
This edition published by Struik Publishers (Pty) Ltd 2000

10 9 8 7 6 5 4 3 2 1

Copyright © text: the authors 1998, 2000
Copyright © colour illustrations: Ken Newman 1998, 2000
Copyright © black and white illustrations: Penny Meakin 1998, 2000
Copyright © published edition: Struik Publishers (Pty) Ltd 2000

Cover and Concept design by Micha McKerr
Typeset by Micha McKerr
Editing and proofreading by Pearson Editorial cc

Reproduction by Positive Proof
Printed and bound by NBD,
Drukkery Street, Goodwood, Western Cape

All rights reserved. No part of this publication may be reproduced,
stored in a retrieval system, or transmitted in any form or by any means,
electronic, mechanical, photocopying, recording or otherwise, without
prior written permission of the copyright holders.

Set in Helvetica 9/11

ISBN 1 86872 552 9

*Users of the book are advised that Guy Gibbon has made available both
audio tapes and CDs of LBJ bird calls as companion productions to this work.*

CONTENTS

Introduction 6

How to use this book 8

How to use this system of identification 9

Step 1: What group of LBJs does the bird belong to? 11
Warblers, robins, chats, bulbuls, honeyguides,
penduline tits, flycatchers and Forest Weaver 11
Larks 12
Pipits 13
Seed-eaters 14

Step 2: Where are you? 32

Step 3: What habitat is the bird in? 33
Woodland 33
Grassland 35
Marshland 36
Fynbos 37
Karoo and semi-arid areas 38
Desert 38
Forest 39
Coastal bush 40
Suburbia 40

Step 4: What time of year is it? 41

Step 5: What species of bird is it? 42

Species descriptions 43
Warblers, robins, chats, bulbuls, honeyguides,
penduline tits, flycatchers and Forest Weaver 43
Larks 90
Pipits 102
Seed-eaters 109

Glossary 130

References 131

Index to scientific names 132

Index to English names 134

• INTRODUCTION •

Flick through the illustrations of any bird field guide and you cannot but notice those pages with a whole lot of lookalike brown birds. Go into the field and it won't be long before you come across half a dozen of these birds which either refuse to look like any particular illustration in the book, or which look just like any of a number of the pictures. Eventually narrow it down to one particular illustration and the distribution map tells you that you are 1 000 kilometres out of this bird's range! Go through this process several times and you are tempted, like many birders, simply to consign these little nondescripts to a great group of untouchables, on which wasting time is pointless.

We all tend to begin our birding careers with that outlook. Unfortunately many birders get stuck there and resolutely ignore the Little Brown Jobs as being impossible. This book aims to give you some hope of cracking the puzzles presented by identifying these LBJs. Fifty years ago the answer was straightforward: "Shoot it, stuff it and send it to Dr Roberts." In those days the only real guide to bird identification was Roberts, Mark I. Admirable though this book was as an introduction to birding in southern Africa, its illustrations did have shortcomings when one tried to sort out nondescript species. But it is nigh impossible to illustrate all these small brown birds in a way that will enable you to determine the identity of your LBJ in the bush. Only after taking a careful look at the text in this book will you begin to appreciate the importance of the habitat preferences and calls of these birds for identification purposes. The best way to identify LBJs is through a process of elimination, as described in this book.

Today the conservation ethic is so strong that collecting is not politically correct. There is, however, a much greater variety of field guides and there are the collections of videos and bird-song recordings. All of these aids need to be used as well as this book.

Why are there so many of these nondescript lookalike birds?

Birds use one of two plumage colour systems. One is to have a distinctive colour or pattern, sometimes even gaudy, and obviously nothing to do with camouflage. Bright colour schemes serve to identify species. The idea is that a bird recognises who to choose as a mate. Getting this right is so important that losing a few individuals to predators does not matter. And the gaudiest members of a gaudy species get the most mates, or at least the first pick, so that in the long term such colour schemes get even brighter.

Note that it is not compulsory for females to be as gaudy as males. Indeed quite often, and nearly always in polygamous species, the females are cryptic, presumably an advantage in remaining inconspicuous in and around the nest.

The alternative system is to rely on song and behaviour to identify a mate. With bright colours now redundant, the ideal plumage is something as cryptic as possible. Predators are something to be reckoned with when all other factors are equal. Habitat is irrelevant: dull or mottled browns or greys are equally inconspicuous in long grass or forest. Cryptic browns and greys are not conducive to producing substantially different patterns, with the result that many small dull-coloured birds look much the same.

We all begin our efforts at identifying the bird in the bush by comparing it with the pictures in a book. For the majority of birds this is fine. For the LBJs that approach is not enough. One of the problems is the fact that the appearance of a number of similar-looking birds on one plate in a book does not mean that those birds live next door to each other in the field: their geographical ranges and habitat preferences may be so different that you will never see them together in the field. The options that seem to present themselves from the illustrations are therefore not always the options that face you in the field.

This book is not going to give you a magic wand to identify every nondescript bird that you come across. Identifying LBJs takes time and experience, but unless you narrow down the options to what is likely to occur where you are doing your birdwatching, you are going to have endless problems in learning to recognise these birds. Bird club outings serve a valuable purpose in this connection. You should be able to sort out half a dozen within a couple of months, but then it becomes more difficult because the next half dozen are likely to occur less frequently or be a lot less vocal. Your elimination process will nevertheless be continuing because, as you recognise the common LBJs in your area, you will be able to eliminate them from the next lot of possibilities that confront you.

You should not expect to recognise every LBJ at all times of the year. When LBJs are not calling they present a far more difficult problem. It is only when you learn to recognise them in the field from constant contact at times when their calls give them away that you can develop any confidence in recognising them when they are not calling.

Identifying LBJs by comparing the bird in the field to illustrations in a book has further complications. There are seasonal changes and there are changes with the age of birds. The fact that the seasonal differences are not all as dramatic as those in the bishops and widows does not mean that they don't exist. Likewise, age differences in LBJs are not as marked as in the hawks and eagles. But when so many species already look alike, the subtleties in the seasonal and age classes have, in the past, led professional ornithologists to think that the juveniles and adults, and the dry and wet season forms of one species were all different species. The grass warblers tend to be a greyer brown in summer and then moult into brighter tawny browns in winter. The juveniles often have a yellowish wash to their plumage. There are also regional differences to contend with. The different forms of some individual species of larks are often far more distinct than the differences between two separate lark species living side by side in their respective ranges. It is these different forms of one species that end up being called "races" or "subspecies". In some cases the pundits are still working out the limits of different species.

• How to use this book •

We have selected about 180 species of birds. Each bird description is cross-referenced to *Newman's Birds of Southern Africa*, 1998 edition. Most birds covered in this book are indisputably small and brown, but a few related species have also been included. This is because, although they have some "obvious" feature, this is not always easily seen in the field. For example, many of the warblers are highly mobile birds, flitting restlessly in the canopy or skulking low down in the undergrowth. It is now that identification, even of distinctively coloured or marked species, becomes difficult. Hence the decision to include some such species in this book.

After several years of birding one grows to realise that it is often easier to sort out nondescript birds by what they have to say and where they live rather than by what they actually look like. So how does one begin to sort out these birds?

By following the five-step elimination process outlined below, and paying careful attention to the bird's call and behaviour – plus plenty of practice – many of the species in this book can be identified, even if you get only a glimpse of the bird.

First prepare an accurate list of those LBJs that occur in your home area, or in the areas you are planning to visit. Distribution maps are indispensable here. The best method is to photocopy the list on the inside front cover of this book and cross off the species that do not occur in your area. Do this while you are working through the various steps in this book and **before** going into the field. You will end up with a considerably reduced list of possibilities for your area. You can repeat this exercise for any area in southern Africa you plan to visit.

Now you are ready to apply the five-step elimination process in the field.

The five-step elimination process

You are outside and looking at a mysterious LBJ. Having checked distribution and noted the bird's habitat and behaviour, then take note of jizz and diagnostic features. These could be a prominent eyebrow, a white tailtip, white outer tail feathers, rufous wing feathers when it flies, etc.

To identify the bird, you apply the five-step elimination process. Each step consists of answering a question:

1 What group of LBJs does the bird belong to?
2 Where are you?
3 What habitat is the bird in?
4 What time of year is it?
5 What species of bird is it?

These steps are now discussed in detail. Remember that if you have drawn up your list of possible LBJs in the area, you have already eliminated a whole number of species. So only the remaining ones come into consideration when **you apply the five steps.**

• How to use this • System of Identification

Before you start

You may find it useful to photocopy the list on the inside cover of the book and use it to eliminate LBJs that are obviously **not** the bird you have seen, and mark those that are **most likely** to be the bird you have seen. Use the steps below to identify which birds should be eliminated and which should be marked.

Step 1

Read the text on pages 11-16 and look at the bill illustrations to decide which group of LBJs your bird belongs to.

Also look at the colour illustrations on pages 17-31 to see whether you can recognise the type of LBJ you have seen.

Once you have eliminated the groups that your bird does not belong to, you should be left with only one list of birds to consider.

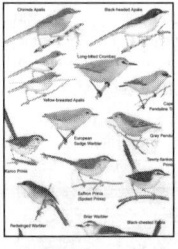
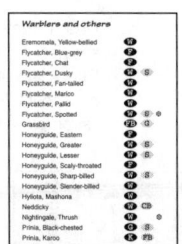

Step 2

Identify the area you are in from the map on page 32; match this to the distribution map when you are looking at the individual species.

Eliminate birds that definitely don't occur in your area from your list.

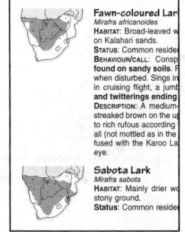
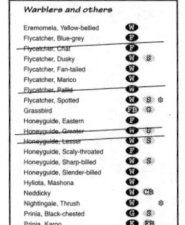

LBJs made easier

Step 3

Use the text and illustrations on pages 33-40 to identify which habitat you have seen the bird in. See which species in the group you have identified favour the habitat you have identified.

Mark all the birds that occur in the identified habitat (bear in mind that birds do not always remain within their preferred habitats and that habitats are sometimes mixed).

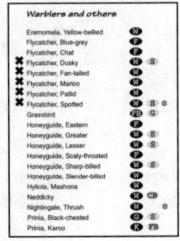

Step 4

Check whether any of the possible species on the list are migrants. Check the times the migrants will be absent from the region in the list on page 41.

Eliminate from your list any birds that are absent during the current month.

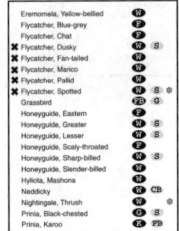

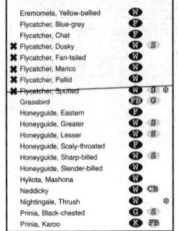

Step 5

Now you need to read the text on the specific species remaining on your list. Look at those marked with the appropriate habitat first. Look for specific identifying characteristics of behaviour, and particularly calls.

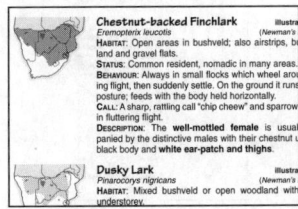

• WHAT GROUP OF LBJS • DOES THE BIRD BELONG TO?

STEP 1

The first step is to determine the group of LBJs to which your mystery bird belongs. For the purposes of this book we have divided the LBJs into four groups:

- Warblers, robins, chats, bulbuls, honeyguides, penduline tits, flycatchers and Forest Weaver
- Larks
- Pipits
- Seed-eaters

The following guidelines will help you assign your LBJ to its correct category.

Warblers, robins, chats, bulbuls, honeyguides, penduline tits, flycatchers and Forest Weaver

The first group is a very mixed bunch, here lumped for convenience.

Warblers are usually very small and dull, and possess distinctive calls. Note, however, that a few are large, and others may be fairly brightly coloured if viewed at close range in good light. What warblers have in common is a thin pointed bill, and the habit of gleaning: inspecting foliage and bark for small insects. Warblers are found in all habitats.

Robins superficially resemble large warblers. However, they have heavier bodies, do much of their gleaning on the ground, and always stay within or near bushy cover. Robins are never found in treeless country.

Chats are related to robins. They have a distinctive upright stance, head held high. Wing-flicking when perched is a typical habit. All food is collected on the ground, usually by gleaning, sometimes by pouncing from a low perch. Most chats are found only in treeless country.

Bulbuls look a bit like warblers, but are generally larger. They forage in all sorts of ways, nearly always in forest or dense cover, and many eat fruit.

Honeyguides also superficially resemble warblers. An obvious feature is their looping flight and the flashing of white outer tail feathers. Pipits also flash white tail feathers, but are typical of open spaces, whereas honeyguides like fairly dense vegetation. At close range the unusual arrangement of the toes of perching honeyguides can be seen: two toes forward, two backward.

Penduline tits resemble minute warblers. Their best character is the habit of gleaning from every position, especially upside-down. Penduline tits move with restless urgency. They are absent from treeless habitats.

Flycatchers have bills slightly flattened from top to bottom. Obvious hairy bristles fringe the sides of the bill. Flycatchers observe the world from an open perch, zooming out at irregular intervals to grab an insect in mid-air. This is called hawking. The grab is accompanied by an audible bill-snap. The victim is then taken back to the perch to be eaten. Flycatchers sometimes pounce directly from this perch onto prey on the ground. Flycatchers require a habitat with trees or bushes at all times.

Black-eyed Bulbul

White-browed Scrub Robin

Rattling Cisticola

Lesser Honeyguide

Larks

Any nondescript, stripy brown bird walking or running on the ground and having a thin bill is likely to be a lark or a pipit. Many larks, however, are primarily seed-eaters and they have shorter, stouter conical bills. Some larks call from elevated perches on bushes or trees, but you never see a lark hopping about and feeding in a tree.

Larks (and pipits) fly in a different way to the other groups. They generally have a leisurely way of moving, with a dipping or undulating flight, and they usually rise well above the ground. Some of them congregate in flocks in the non-breeding season but the flocks are loose-knit and poorly coordinated.

Larks are usually regarded as a highly confusing group of terrestrial LBJs and are seldom given a second glance by the faint-hearted. There is no magic formula for larks, but many can be identified with a fair degree of accuracy, not by plumage alone but by habitat, song and behaviour. As with most LBJs, determination and patience are required. The first step is to be sure that you are looking at a lark and not a member of some other group.

What makes a lark a lark?

- Larks spend most of their day on the ground unless singing, in which case they will be either flying or perched on some low bush, termite mound, rock

What group of LBJs?

or fence post. Singing mostly takes place in early summer and is an integral part of a lark's territorial display during the breeding season.

- Larks **run** on the ground (they don't hop) and they run **between** the grass tufts, not over them as do some pipits. Most larks will accept a motor vehicle at close range, but are likely to flush from a person walking, therefore stay in your motor vehicle if you want to get close. Larks have a dipping flight.
- Most larks have fairly stout bills; they eat a lot of seeds. The bill is seldom more than half the length of the bird's head. The upper ridge of the bill (the culmen) is rounded. Longer bills are seen only in the Spike-heeled and Long-billed Larks (*Newman's Birds* p. 283), since they eat more insects than grain.
- Many larks (14 out of 23) have some degree of dark spotting on the upper breast.
- Most (20 out of 23) have pale underparts, either whitish, creamy or buffy. Only the three male finchlarks (*Newman's Birds* p. 287) are black below.
- In most larks the sexes are alike.
- Larks with a wide distribution have richer plumage in the east and paler plumage in the west; they may even have other regional plumage variations.

Thick-billed Lark

Spike-heeled Lark

Pipits

Even more than the larks, the pipits are a notoriously difficult group of birds to sort out, and are often misidentified even by the experts. As is the case with larks, a combination of factors such as song, behaviour and habitat is more important than plumage characteristics when trying to identify pipits, and the best time to start learning about them is during the breeding season when all of these points come into play.

Like larks, pipits are terrestrial birds but some of them, particularly the Tree Pipit, Wood Pipit and Striped Pipit, often fly up into a tree and may walk about on the main branches. The Bushveld Pipit also goes into trees. But pipits never move through a tree like a Puffback Shrike or a Southern Black Tit.

What makes a pipit a pipit?

- Pipits (like larks) spend most of their time on the ground. Most species sing from a low perch such as a bush or rock, or even from the ground, but only a few have a display flight during which they sing.

- Pipits also run along the ground (and do not hop), although a few woodland species walk in a purposeful manner rather than run. Most pipits run a short distance, then pause and wag their tails up and down, some more obviously than others. They scramble over grass tufts or rocks. Some of the grassland species fly reluctantly when approached, preferring to hide among the grass tufts until the last minute. They then fly some distance before settling into the grass again. Woodland pipits fly up into the trees when disturbed.
- Pipits are insect eaters, and therefore have fairly long and slender bills. Their legs are also long to enable them to run in the grassland or woodland.
- Most pipits (nine of 12) show dark streaking or blotching on the back, and two of these are small birds, which is a further aid to identification. The other three have plain backs.
- Most species are streaked on the breast, but the intensity varies from heavy to light streaking depending on the species, and in some this is so faint that it is difficult to see in the field.
- The outer tail feathers of the 12 species are either white or buff in colour, and this can be useful when trying to distinguish between species that occur in similar habitats.

Grassveld Pipit

Long-billed Pipit

In the field the above features can be used to separate the different species of pipits, and you should take careful note of all these characters. Finally, pay close attention to the habitat in which each pipit is found, whether open grassland, cultivated fields, rocky hillsides, woodland, floodplains and so on.

Seed-eaters

The most distinctive feature of these birds is their bills, which are shorter and stronger than those of most larks or pipits. They also have a chunkier body build. But it is their behaviour that really sets them apart.

They move with much more purpose and precision than other nondescript birds and they often form big, organised flocks. This applies particularly to the weavers and their close relatives; the sparrows and canaries are less inclined to gather in large flocks. Be careful about species that are normally associated with open areas. They can move into woodland in spring and feed in the canopy as part of a mixed bird party consisting of several different species.

This major group includes the females, non-breeding males and juveniles of weavers, bishops, widows, queleas, whydahs and widow finches, as well as sparrows, brown canaries and siskins.

Red Bishop (f)

Streaky-headed Canary

Spotted-backed weaver (f)

Cape Sparrow (f)

Female and non-breeding weavers

All weavers have the heavy bill typical of seed-eaters. With few exceptions weavers are larger than other seed-eaters. The majority of female weavers are variably yellow, paler below, darker and duller above. Colour is not constant throughout the year, and there is a semblance of "breeding dress" when the females become slightly brighter and yellower. Male weavers start life looking like females, and most do not assume their first breeding plumage until they are two years old. However, they may gradually acquire some adult features during these two years, for example eye colour. In subsequent adult life males moult their breeding finery once a year, to spend winters in eclipse plumage virtually identical to that of the females. With a few exceptions, weavers have harsh calls that do not aid identification.

Female and non-breeding bishops, widows and queleas

This is a fairly uniform lot. Generally they are slightly smaller than the "true" weavers, with shorter and relatively deeper bills. The eye is invariably brown; legs are pinkish brown. All species are a dull greyish brown above with a mottled effect created by paler edges to the back feathers. There is an obvious supercilium: a pale eyebrow stripe above the eye. The underparts range from off-white to buff, with or without streaking. In all species males moult from breeding dress to an eclipse plumage which either resembles that of females exactly or retains some elements of the breeding dress. In most species males first breed at age two, females at one. All species have similar calls, not much use in identification.

Female and non-breeding whydahs and widow finches

All southern African species are closely related, and this is reflected in the great similarity of the females. All are small, compactly built, and have a very short conical bill. The eye is invariably brown. The upperparts are various shades of dull brown, most feathers having paler edges, creating a scaled effect. The head is striped, the crown stripe being the same colour as the eyebrow stripe; darker stripes separate them and may also extend backwards from the eye. Non-breeding males moult into an eclipse plumage very similar to that of the females. Juveniles – fledglings that have not yet acquired any adult plumage – are an almost uniform smoky brown, paler below. Virtually the same plumage is seen in some mannikins, waxbills and firefinches. Since this plumage has no diagnostic value it will receive no further treatment.

Whydahs and widow finches all have a characteristic foraging behaviour, hopping forward and scratching the ground as they land, and inspecting their handiwork. When breeding, all are brood parasites, ecologically tied to their hosts. Since the host-parasite relationship is often specific, the presence of the host sometimes assists identification of the parasite.

Sparrows

In general body dimensions, sparrows most closely resemble the smaller female widows. The differences are subtle: sparrows have very slightly shorter bills and longer tails. Sparrows have predominantly brown upperparts, the underparts being off-white to pale grey, sometimes with a hint of brown. The most obvious unifying feature of sparrow plumage is the white bar(s) on the wing, formed by the alignment of pale tips to the wing coverts. The eyes are invariably dark; the legs are various shades of dull pinkish brown.

Brown canaries

In addition to the six yellow canaries, there are also six brown canaries in southern Africa. Two are easily identified, while four qualify as LBJs. At first glance these birds appear sparrow-like, their bills being fairly short and broad-based. Canaries sing from the top of a tree but, being primarily seed-eaters, they feed mostly on the ground or on grass-heads.

Siskins are a type of small canary and the two species that concern us are dull birds mostly confined to montane regions. They do not have attractive songs.

Illustrations not to scale

• WHERE ARE YOU? •
STEP 2

Your position on the map of southern Africa determines what you are likely to see. In Cape Town you are not going to find everything that you will see in Zimbabwe, and if you are in Windhoek or Walvis Bay you won't find most of what there is to see in Durban or Dundee across in KwaZulu-Natal. In fact if you are in Dundee you will have very different birds to those in Durban even though both places are in the same province. This is attributable to differences in altitude and habitat rather than the geographical range of birds.

The southern African region

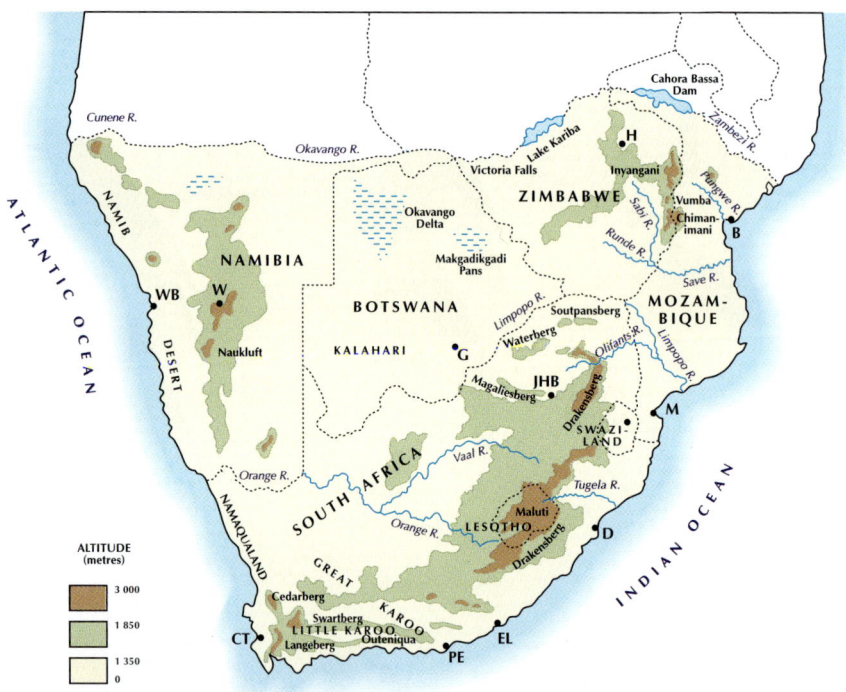

Note: Residents and migrants

The distribution maps show dark shading for resident birds and pale shading for migrants.

• WHAT HABITAT • IS THE BIRD IN?
STEP 3

The arrangement of this book is to classify birds by group first and then by habitat. In this book the habitats are broken down into nine principal categories, some with several subcategories. These will not all exist in your target area. There is no fynbos in Zimbabwe and there is no evergreen forest in the Kalahari. But Zimbabwe does have fynbos birds such as the Neddicky, and some birds are not too fussed by differences in habitat. But there are lots of birds that have very definite habitat preferences.

Learn to recognise the habitat that you are in, and get to know which kinds of birds you are likely to see in that particular habitat. However, the dividing lines between the different habitats described here may not always be easy to recognise in practice. Also, habitats that are significantly different sometimes occur in a jumbled mosaic. And the trouble is that birds have wings, so they are much more mobile than most living creatures. This means that birds which this book slots into a particular habitat may be found in a habitat for which they are not listed because they are crossing from one habitat island to the next one. The book nevertheless aims to give a good general guide of what sort of countryside will support what sort of birds most of the time.

When you make your local list, leave a number of columns for the habitats that occur in your vicinity, and tick off the habitats in which each of your list of potentials is most likely to occur. Alternatively arrange the list in habitat order and put noughts and crosses against your "summer only" and "winter only" birds.

The following abbreviations are used in this book for the main habitats:

- **W** woodland
- **G** grassland
- **M** marshland
- **FB** fynbos
- **K** Karoo and semi-arid areas
- **D** desert
- **F** forest
- **CB** coastal bush
- **S** suburbia

Woodland **W**

Woodland is here defined as a woody community ranging from savanna scrub to riverine forest. Savanna scrub can be a mosaic of bush patches, grading, where soil depth or rainfall permits, into open woodland. Riverine forest is easily recognised as a bright green swathe in an area of otherwise dry deciduous woodland. It has some features in common with true forest, but is included here because its birds are most likely to be seen alongside woodland birds. Many types of LBJs occur in woodland.

Ecologically, woodland differs from forest in that the tree canopy is not contiguous; indeed it may be very sparse. There is plenty of light at ground level, grass can grow, and in the dry season grass fires are likely. So all woodland trees are fire-resistant once past the seedling stage. Most are deciduous and therefore well equipped to withstand drought.

Thickets are low-growing, near-impenetrable bushy clumps usually found on termite mounds or along dry riverbeds. They are an especially important feature of woodland.

Woodland is often further defined by other names: "broad-leaved" means woodland with few or no acacias, while "thornveld" is woodland dominated by acacias. Although there are many species of indigenous acacias, only a few ever become dominant, and in any one area most of the acacias will be of a single species. In the warmer northern areas the dominant species is often *Acacia nigrescens;* in Zululand it may be *A. tortilis*; further south *A. sieberiana* or *A. nilotica*; with *A. karroo* dominating thornveld where winters are cold.

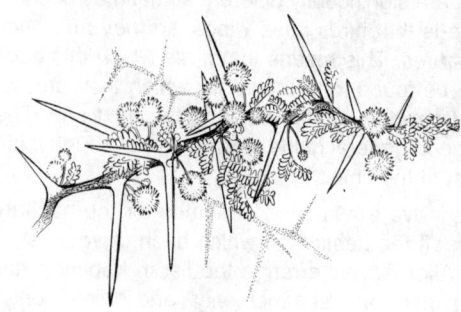
Detail of acacia twig with thorns and leaves

Cross-section of typical thornveld habitat

Broad-leaved communities are often diverse. Broad-leaved woodland in Zimbabwe is dominated by what is called miombo: species of *Julbernardia* and *Brachystegia*, with *Colophospermum mopane* at lower altitudes. The mopane extends into South Africa but is replaced to the south by *Sclerocarya birrea* (marula) or by species of *Combretum* or *Terminalia*, especially where the soil is sandy.

Cross-section of typical broad-leaved woodland habitat

Riverine forest is altogether different. It forms strips along major rivers and contains mainly trees that can survive or withstand being knocked over by floods. Since they subsist mainly on groundwater supplied from a distant catchment, they can remain evergreen without high local rainfall. Riverine forest may extend far into dry country. Typical trees are *Trichilia emetica, Ficus sycomorus, Acacia xanthophloea* and *Breonadia microcephala*.

Detail of typical miombo twig with leaves   *Detail of mopane leaves*

Grassland ⓖ

Grassland is a fire-dominated habitat which occurs from sea-level to high mountain tops, provided that rainfall is adequate and that most rain falls in summer. Light to moderate grazing helps to maintain grassland because grass is not damaged by being cut back: its growing point is at ground level. By contrast, grazing sets back seedling shrubs and trees by constantly removing the growing points. Heavy grazing, paradoxically, favours tree invasion because very short grass cannot catch fire, and any seedlings the grazers spare can grow to a fire-proof size. Without constant maintenance grassland tends to revert to evergreen forest in wet areas, to dry woodland in hot areas, and to Karoo vegetation in dry areas.

The diversity of grass species and of grass communities in southern Africa is very high. Nevertheless, relatively few species are both common and widespread; examples are *Themeda triandra, Tristachya hispida, Heteropogon contortus, Eragrostis racemosa, Setaria flabellata* and *Aristida junciformis*. Birds are scarcely affected by the species composition of grassland; the structure nearly

Cross-section of typical grassland habitat grading into woodland

always determines which birds will be present: warblers, larks, pipits and seed-eaters are very common, while several chats also occur. Structure is influenced not only by the current stage in the grazing or burning cycle, but by the presence or absence of tiny shrubs, termite mounds and seasonally wet spots.

The following terms are used to describe grassland: "very short" means below ankle height; "short" means ankle to knee height; "long" means knee to head height and "tall" means above head height.

Marshland

Cross-section of typical marshland habitat

Marshland is a wetland, usually with water underfoot. It often occurs on the fringes of dams, below dam walls and along the edges of streams and rivers, and intergrades with the tall grass subhabitats of grassland and sometimes with short matted grassland.

Natural marshes tend to occur in one of two situations. In the midlands or uplands the catchment of a river headwater often consists of marshes on small flat areas before the river sets off on its permanently flowing downhill course. Near sea-level, especially on the flat plain of the south-eastern coast, rivers lose momentum and may spread out as they deposit some of their silt. Occasionally, somewhere between these two extremes, a river meanders across the floor of a broad valley, leaving behind oxbows and soggy hollows that also support typical marsh vegetation.

Marshland is home to many warblers and seed-eaters, but no other LBJs.

Artificial habitats may also have marshy areas – dam fringes and seepages below dam walls – and marshes may intergrade with dry grassland. Depending upon the depth and permanence of the water, and soil characteristics, a variety of marshland plant communities may be encountered:

- Reed-beds, which can be 3 m and more tall, and very extensive, consist mainly of *Phragmites* species, which have long pointed leaves and big fluffy flower heads.
- Bulrushes, of the genus *Typha*, have tall, smooth, strap-like leaves, with cylindrical chocolate lollipop flowering heads that break down into a fluffy mass.
- Sedge marshes can be diverse. Sedges have three-angled stems, common species being *Carex, Scirpus, Eleocharis* and *Cyperus*. *Merxmuellera* is a grass that likes this habitat.
- Rush marshes are usually dominated by *Juncus*, which has smooth rounded stems, few or apparently no leaves and insignificant flowers.

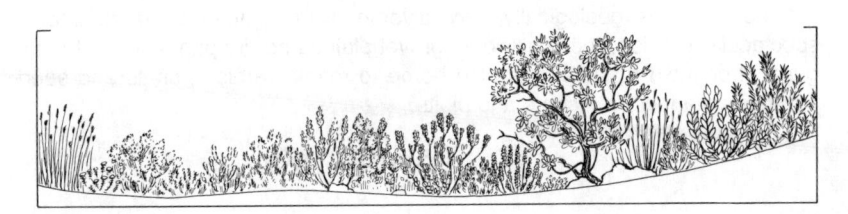

Fynbos **FB**

Cross-section of typical fynbos habitat

True fynbos is restricted to the winter-rainfall area of the south-western Cape. Winter rain tends to exclude both grass – which requires surface water in summer, the growing season – and forest trees – which suffer in fires in the hot dry summer. Fynbos plants combine the ability to use water from lower soil levels in the growing season with fire resistance, even fire dependence. Nearly all the plants are bushes, common examples being species of *Protea, Leucospermum, Leucadendron, Erica* and the grass-like family Restionaceae. Fynbos usually grows on very coarse, sandy, acid soil.

The term fynbos is also applied to the low-growing bushy scrub that replaces grass in overgrazed spots on the damper parts of mountains to the east and north of true fynbos. Typical plants are species of *Phylica, Cliffortia, Passerina, Metalasia, Euryops* and *Felicia*. Some fynbos birds use this vegetation, responding more to its structure than to its plant composition.

Fynbos is noted for its shortage of birds altogether. A few warblers, chats and seed-eaters are common.

Karoo and semi-arid areas Ⓚ

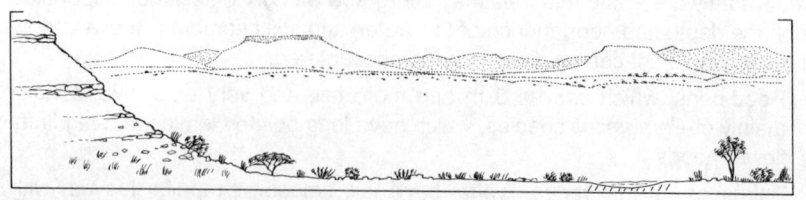

Cross-section of typical Karoo or semi-arid grassland habitat

The Karoo occupies a large part of the South African interior, being bounded in the south and west by fynbos, in the north by dry woodland and in the east by grassland. Originally the Karoo was predominantly dry grassland, but 200 years of overgrazing have virtually eliminated the grassy component. Now small scattered shrubs are the most obvious plants, common examples being species of *Pentzia, Eriocephalus, Zygophyllum, Pteronia* and *Lycium*. Typical Karoo trees are *Acacia karroo, Rhus lancea, R. undulata* and *Rhigozum obovatum*. Some areas of the Karoo are famous for their endemic succulents, many of which are vygies belonging to the family Mesembryanthemaceae.

The Karoo is geologically very diverse, with its flat-topped mountains, spectacular erosion, rocky hillsides, gravel plains and dry pan fringes. It is the great stronghold of larks; it is also home to many warblers, chats and seed-eaters, and a few flycatchers and pipits.

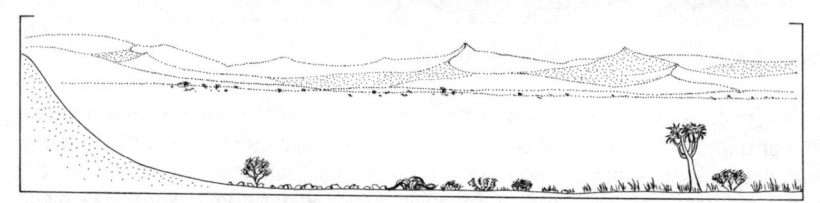

Desert Ⓓ

Cross-section of typical desert habitat

True desert is confined to the extreme west of the subregion, extending from the Northern Cape along the whole coastal strip of Namibia. In most years there is no rain at all, and the main source of moisture is coastal fog. There are two main habitats. Shifting sand dunes, which are normally devoid of vegetation, nevertheless support an interesting fauna, including several larks. Wind-blown plant debris is the principal food source for this system. The second main habitat consists of gravel plains and rocky hills with some grass (usually species of *Stipagrostis*) and a few trees and succulents. Prominent are *Euphorbia virosa, Aloe dichotoma* and species of *Commiphora*. Typical desert trees are *Acacia albida, A. erioloba* and *Euclea pseudebenus*. Larks and chats are typical of open desert.

Forest F

Cross-section of typical evergreen forest habitat

Evergreen forest is an indigenous tree community in which the canopies interlock. It must not be confused with commercial timber plantations of exotic pine or eucalyptus trees whose canopies also interlock but which support few birds. Within an indigenous forest sunlight penetration to the lower levels is naturally limited, resulting in a cool, shaded interior. Since evergreen forests normally grow in regions of high rainfall, many shade and moisture-loving mosses, ferns and orchids flourish on the trees. These moist tree habitats are found in two major zones in the south and east of the subregion. They are the warm lowland evergreen forests such as are found near the coast of the Southern and Eastern Cape, KwaZulu-Natal and Mozambique, and the cool, high-altitude evergreen forests on the mistbelt and mountain slopes of the eastern escarpment at altitudes of up to 2 000 metres.

So diverse is lowland forest that there is no such thing as a typical community. However, common and widespread trees include *Ficus natalensis, Albizia adianthifolia, Bridelia micrantha, Protorhus longifolia, Trema orientalis, Englerophytum natalense* and *Antidesma venosum*. Cool inland forests are totally different. Unexploited forests are dominated by yellowwoods such as *Podocarpus latifolius* and *P. falcatus*, and the Sneezewood *Ptaeroxylon obliquum*; when these are removed *Celtis africana, Xymalos monospora, Combretum kraussii* and *Kiggelaria africana* become more obvious. Zimbabwe highland forests have their own characteristic species such as *Polyscias fulva, Harungana madagascariensis* and *Ficus exasperata*.

Beneath the high tree canopy of an evergreen forest the substorey is fairly open, consisting mainly of the bare trunks of mature trees plus slender saplings reaching upwards. Along forest streams and in clearings there may be patches of grasses and small flowering shrubs, even thickets. Birdlife within the forest is mostly found high in the canopy or just beneath it, making detection of species difficult. Some birds, such as certain robins, bulbuls and warblers, prefer to forage in the leaf litter on the ground, but may be difficult to approach.

An important element of evergreen forests is the forest fringe or edge. The fringe is often dense and almost impenetrable, consisting of small to medium pioneer trees and tangled creepers. It is frequented by not only the true forest birds but also by many other species from adjoining, non-forest habitats, including especially sunbirds, warblers and waxbills. Conversely, true forest birds regularly extend their foraging ranges up to 200 metres from the forest fringe into adjacent bush or nearby gardens. These are opportunistic, short-term forays away from their prime habitat.

Coastal bush (CB)

Cross-section of typical coastal bush habitat

Coastal bush, as seen on the dunes fringing much of the eastern coastline, is a very dense, windswept bush and tree community growing to a maximum height of some 4-5 metres; usually not more than 3 metres. Beyond these heights it qualifies for the name "dune forest", as occurs on the northern coast. In coastal bush the tree canopies interlock in the middle stratum and are almost impenetrable.

In the southern Cape common components of coastal bush are *Rhus glauca, R. crenata, Diospyros dichrophylla* and *Cussonia thyrsiflora*. Further east the community becomes very diverse, including *Eugenia capensis, Aloe thraskii, Allophylus natalensis, Chrysanthemoides monilifera, Ficus burtt-davyi* and *Strelitzia nicolai*.

This dense habitat is frequented by several LBJs including bulbul species, warblers and flycatchers in addition to more colourful species.

Suburbia (S)

This term refers to wooded parks and gardens. A new suburb becomes a mixed, open woodland within a few years as a result of planting and regular irrigation. After about 20 years it contains many mature trees. Individual gardens often have corners of dense bush, even thickets. These well-watered, insect-rich habitats are highly attractive to many birds including weavers, sparrows, robins, bulbuls and flycatchers and have an added influx of migrant warblers in summer. The average mature suburban garden can boast an annual bird species count of between 30 and 45, according to region.

• What time of year is it? •
Step 4

Everyone knows that many kinds of swallows migrate and are here only in summer. So too do lots of waders, storks and brown eagles. But one does not necessarily think of an LBJ like a Willow Warbler, which weighs only about 9 grams, migrating from Siberia to the Cape and back.

And it is not only the intercontinental migrants that one has to think about. Many birds migrate within Africa. Several of these are essentially altitudinal migrants, moving down from the mountains or highveld to warmer places at lower levels in winter. Others tend to move from east to west and back again to avoid or follow exceptionally wet or dry seasons.

So check **when** certain birds are likely to move out of your area. Then mark up your lists to reflect when those that occur within your geographical range are going to be here or away. There will always be early arrivals and late departures but put them out of your mind until you have become reasonably confident about recognising particular migrants when there are plenty of them about. Don't be surprised to find that you have winter only birds as well as summer only ones. The migrants are:

Warblers:	**Months absent from region:**
African Marsh Warbler	Mid-April to late September
European Marsh Warbler	Mid-April to late September
European Sedge Warbler	Mid-April to late September
Garden Warbler	Mid-April to late September
Great Reed Warbler	Mid-April to late September
Icterine Warbler	Mid-April to late September
Olive-tree Warbler	March to late October
River Warbler	March to late October
Spotted Flycatcher	April to September
Thrush Nightingale	March/April to December
Whitethroat	April to October
Willow Warbler	April to September

Lark:	
Dusky Lark	May to October

Pipits:	
Mountain Pipit	March to mid-October
Tree Pipit	May to September

Seed-eater:	
Red-headed Quelea	April to September

• What species • of bird is it?
Step 5

Once you have slotted your bird into its correct group and habitat, appearance often has limited further use. It is the bird's specific or individual behaviour and, more particularly, its call that will now tell you what the bird is.

But even then things are not simple. It is virtually impossible to adequately describe a bird's call in words. You therefore have to learn the calls from recordings. A Fan-tailed Cisticola, for example, has a very distinctive call and behaviour, and the calls described are virtually the whole of its repertoire. But you must realise that the calls described or recorded are often only some of the calls that a particular bird makes. Many other species have quite an array of different calls, and only its characteristic "signature tune" is described. Be sure to learn this, because the bird will probably give you a rendition and so reveal its identity.

Matters are further complicated by the fact that some birds are mostly silent for the greater part of the year. You therefore need to learn to recognise the bird when it is calling. You may initially be able to identify it only between Christmas and Easter. That's better than never recognising it at all. By the next year you may have forgotten the call, but as time goes on it should become familiar and you will begin to recognise the jizz of the bird and some of its other calls. You may eventually recognise the species without too much difficulty even when it does not have much to say.

Finally, you need to realise that the calls or displays of some birds vary from one region to another. In the Mashonaland province of Zimbabwe, Ayres' Cisticola has two lows and two highs in its call. In Gauteng it has one low and three highs. The Flappet Lark has a display which seems reasonably distinctive, but there are several variations on the theme of volleys of flapping: in some places the bird performs two short volleys and then a long one, but in other areas a couple of longs followed by a couple of shorts. So do not think that because you know a Lazy Cisticola in KwaZulu-Natal you are going to recognise it straightaway in Zimbabwe.

• Warblers, Robins, • Chats, Bulbuls, Honey-guides, Penduline Tits, Flycatchers and Forest Weaver

Woodland

───── Canopy of broad-leaved woodland ─────

Broad-leaved tree: canopy and mid-level

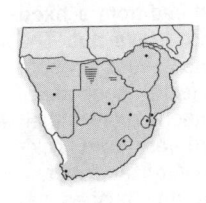

Willow Warbler
Phylloscopus trochilus

illustrated page 19
(*Newman's Birds* p. 333)

Habitat: All kinds of woodland, both broad-leaved and thornveld, forest edges and even gardens. Less commonly recorded in arid regions, where it is confined to areas with adequate tree cover.
Status: Very common non-breeding summer visitor, occurring from October to April.
Behaviour: Often seen singly but some races go about in loose formations of six or more. Feeds actively in the outer canopy or middle section of trees and bushes, gleaning insects off the leaves and twigs.
Call: A cascading warble of about 25 notes, like a white-eye but descending and fading; heard mostly just after its arrival in October to December and prior to its departure in late March to April. More usual is a short single or double note "suet" or "sweet" given at intervals of 1-30 seconds.
Description: Most are overall greenish yellow but some races are brown above and paler below, sometimes almost white. It has an eye-stripe and a notch in the tailtip.

Grey Penduline Tit
Anthoscopus caroli

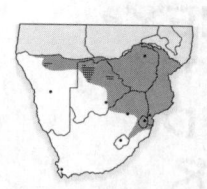

illustrated page 21
(*Newman's Birds* p. 345)

HABITAT: Mainly broad-leaved woodland, but also thornveld in areas where the Cape Penduline Tit does not occur.
STATUS: Common resident.
BEHAVIOUR: Found in groups of 4-8 in the tree-tops, often around flowers. They float in straggling procession (follow-my-leader) from one tree-top to the next.
CALL: Similar to that of the Common Waxbill "ChikChikZEE, ChikChikZEE, ChikChikZEE, ChikChikZEE"; emphasis on the last syllable.
DESCRIPTION: A tiny grey bird with a buff or rufous facial mask and belly.

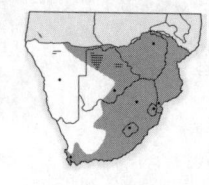

Neddicky
Cisticola fulvicapilla

illustrated page 24
(*Newman's Birds* p. 353)

HABITAT: Broad-leaved woodland throughout the subregion with the exception of the far west. Comes to vlei edges or into ecotones where there are scattered bushes. Also occurs in montane areas of the south-western Cape.
STATUS: Common resident.
BEHAVIOUR/CALL: It calls in the canopy and feeds in the understorey. Hops about on the ground, in low bushes and tufts of grass under woodland canopy. Also comes out into more open scrub and savanna, short grass and sparse cover. Seen in the canopy when it calls "chirri-chirri-chirri" (not unlike Stierling's Barred Warbler). This is a territorial call uttered from a **fixed perch at the top of a tree where the bird stays put.** The song is a high-pitched note repeated for long periods at about three per second, like a tinker barbet but faster "seep-seep-seep-seep". The alarm call sounds like someone running their fingers through the teeth of a comb, but **not very loud** "ticki-ticki-ticki-ticki" in little bursts about 10-12 very rapid notes. Often two birds give this call, which is heard from bushes and lower parts of trees.
DESCRIPTION: A very small cisticola with a **plain back and no spots at the tailtip**. The conspicuous rufous cap contrasts with the back. The southern and eastern races have blue-grey underparts whereas the northern races have pale brown underparts.

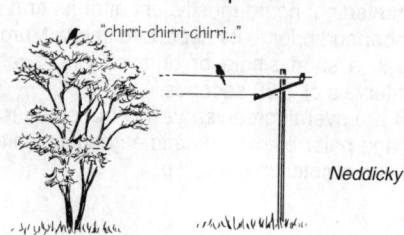

Neddicky

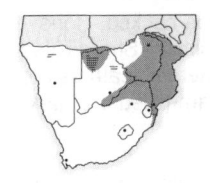

Fan-tailed Flycatcher
Myioparus plumbeus

illustrated page 28
(*Newman's Birds* p. 363)

HABITAT: Broad-leaved woodland and riparian forest.
STATUS: Uncommon resident.
BEHAVIOUR: Usually heard before it is seen. A highly active and conspicuous species with totally different behaviour to the otherwise similar Blue-grey Flycatcher. It is not a still-hunter, but forages by moving steadily through the mid-stratum of tree canopies, gleaning insects from leaves while giving its far-carrying call. **Repeatedly raises and lowers its fanned tail.**
CALL: A far-carrying "tree-reee".
DESCRIPTION: **The fanned tail is conspicuously black with white outer tail feathers.** The immature has spotted upperparts and mottled underparts.

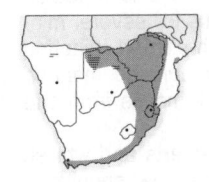

Sharp-billed Honeyguide
Prodotiscus regulus

illustrated page 17
(*Newman's Birds* p. 275)

HABITAT: Open woodland, forest edges, exotic plantations and gardens.
STATUS: Uncommon resident.
BEHAVIOUR/CALL: Usually perches high in a tree. It is easily overlooked. Often performs complicated aerial manoeuvres at lower levels, at which time it utters a thin "tseet" and **its white rump and white outer tail feathers can be seen**. To call, it will settle on a tree-top and **peer slowly from side to side while bobbing its head up and down.** Then it utters a thin, tinkling note that resembles a weak version of the Crested Barbet's call "tirrrrrrrrr", after which it flies off directly.
DESCRIPTION: A restless little greyish bird with a slender bill. Easily confused with the small flycatchers such as the Spotted and Dusky, as well as with the Slender-billed Honeyguide, but has a browner back in comparison with the greenish back of the Slender-billed.

Slender-billed Honeyguide
Prodotiscus zambesiae

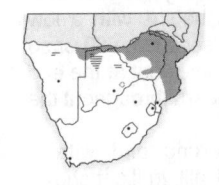

illustrated page 17
(*Newman's Birds* p. 275)

HABITAT: Broad-leaved woodland in the higher altitudes of Zimbabwe; also similar habitat in northern Botswana and neighbouring Namibia.
STATUS: Uncommon resident.
BEHAVIOUR: Small, rather inconspicuous and therefore not often seen. Very warbler-like in both appearance and behaviour. It feeds by gleaning off the bark and leaves, and flies out to hawk passing insects. It has a **distinctive undulating display flight**, executed above the canopy. During the flight it often fans its tail, showing off the characteristic **white outer tail feathers**.
CALL: While displaying it gives a harsh call "skeee-aa", which is repeated over and over.

DESCRIPTION: The alternative name, Green-backed Honeyguide, helps to separate it from the very similar Sharp-billed Honeyguide which is browner above. Its outer tail feathers are completely white whereas those of the Sharp-billed are dark-tipped on the corners and base.

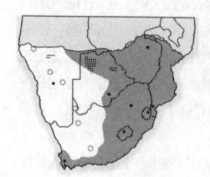

Greater Honeyguide
Indicator indicator

illustrated page 17
(*Newman's Birds* p. 273)

HABITAT: Open woodland, wooded hillsides, riparian forest and well-wooded suburbia.
STATUS: Common resident.
BEHAVIOUR/CALL: A canopy bird. Very difficult to locate unless calling. The male uses a regular call-site during the summer months from where it utters a far-carrying "WHIT-purr" or "VICtorr", with the accent on the first syllable. This is repeated monotonously at about 1,5 second intervals for several minutes at a time. When guiding it makes a high-pitched chittering sound and flutters about in a restless or agitated manner, showing off its white outer tail feathers as it moves from one perch to another nearby.
DESCRIPTION: Both sexes have brown upperparts and whitish underparts, with pale cheek-patches and yellow shoulders. The male is told by the **black throat and pink bill**, the female by the white throat and black bill. The immature is brown above and yellow below. In flight **all age groups show white outer tail feathers**.

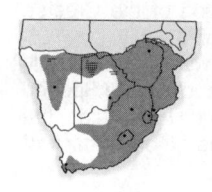

Lesser Honeyguide
Indicator minor

illustrated page 17
(*Newman's Birds* p. 273)

HABITAT: Wooded habitats with tall trees, often exotics; also gardens.
STATUS: Common resident.
BEHAVIOUR/CALL: Generally seen singly. Easily overlooked unless calling. Calls for much of the year from a high, regular call-perch, often in a blue-gum tree. The call begins with a low "chrr", followed at intervals of a bit under a second by 30 or so single-syllable notes, each of which rises somewhat at the end "chrr ... trit, trit, trit, trit ...". This call can be heard throughout the day.
DESCRIPTION: An inconspicuous, grey-looking bird with a yellow-green back and a fairly stubby black bill. In flight shows **white outer tail feathers**.

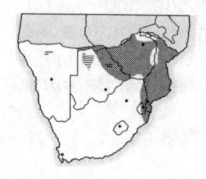

Stierling's Barred Warbler
Calamonastes stierlingi

illustrated page 22
(*Newman's Birds* p. 347)

HABITAT: Broad-leaved woodland, particularly miombo.
STATUS: Common resident.
BEHAVIOUR: Lives two lives. (a) In summer the male calls high in the canopy. The call is **uttered from a fixed perch at the**

top of a tree from which the bird doesn't move much. (b) Forages on the ground in low bushes and at the edge of thickets where it moves around slowly. Also has a butterfly-like display flight below the woodland canopy with exaggerated but slow wing-flaps.

CALL: A high-pitched and monotonous "birribit, birribit, birribit". Each phrase has a bit of a roll and successive phrases follow each other quickly: about two phrases per second, and continuing for 30 seconds at a time before pausing and then resuming. A common woodland sound.

DESCRIPTION: White underparts with black bars from chin to vent distinctive.

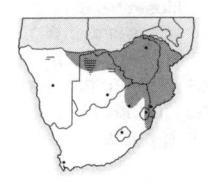

Green-capped Eremomela
Eremomela scotops

illustrated page 22
(*Newman's Birds* p. 345)

HABITAT: Mainly broad-leaved woodland (particularly miombo in Zimbabwe); also riverine woodland.
STATUS: Common resident.
BEHAVIOUR: Always found in small groups of 4-8. Very territorial in the group and noisy when groups meet on edges of territories. A bird party specialist.
CALL: Two distinct calls, quite unlike each other and given at different times of the day. Before sunrise a single bird, perhaps the alpha male of the group, calls for extended periods from a fixed spot: a loud bisyllabic "twip-twip" at about three per second. Thereafter a **husky chattering** is uttered by all members of the small family party as they move through the tree-tops.
DESCRIPTION: A two-tone bird, grey-green above and yellow below. The dark upperparts are clearly separate from the paler underparts. The eyes are pale yellow.

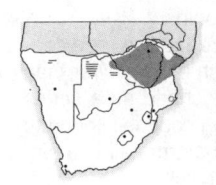

Red-faced Crombec
Sylvietta whytii

illustrated page 24
(*Newman's Birds* p. 343)

HABITAT: Mainly broad-leaved woodland in Zimbabwe and parts of Mozambique.
STATUS: Uncommon resident.
BEHAVIOUR: Found in pairs and joins bird parties, feeding in an active, jerky manner in the canopy.
CALL: Characteristic call is a series of 12-15 notes that slowly rise in pitch and take 2-3 seconds to get through. A background sound, unlike the more strident call of the common Long-billed Crombec. Also has a "chik" contact call.
DESCRIPTION: **Very short tail and no eye-stripe.** The bird is grey above and rufous below.

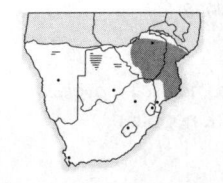

Mashona Hyliota
Hyliota australis

illustrated page 28
(*Newman's Birds* p. 361)

HABITAT: **Restricted to the canopy of broad-leaved woodland** in Zimbabwe and Mozambique.

STATUS: Uncommon resident.
BEHAVIOUR: Very active but easily overlooked in the canopy. Usually in pairs or small family groups; joins mixed bird parties. Very territorial, holding a territory throughout the year. Often chases other birds.
CALL: A two-syllabled chippering whistle and a trilling warble. The contact call is a high-pitched "tick ... tick" given at intervals of 1-2 seconds.
DESCRIPTION: A black and pale yellow bird, very similar to the Yellow-breasted Hyliota but has a **matt black back** (Yellow-breasted has a glossy black back).

Short-winged Cisticola
Cisticola brachyptera

illustrated page 24
(*Newman's Birds* p. 353)

HABITAT: Restricted to the east of Zimbabwe in areas such as the Honde Valley, Haroni-Rusitu Botanical Reserves and around Mount Selinda, where it can be found in well-developed woodland with dead trees for calling posts.
STATUS: Uncommon resident.
BEHAVIOUR: Male sings from the top of a dead tree and also has an aerial display, but forages in the grass and bush below the canopy. In the Honde Valley around Katiyo Tea Estate it calls from the top of a *Borassus* palm and forages in the tea plantation below. Also performs an aerial cruise, high up like an Ayres' or Cloud Cisticola, ending with a spectacular dive back to the ground, but the song, if any, is too weak to hear from down below.
CALL: A series of three to five "see-see-see-see" notes, each a little lower than the one before. Described as a series of very weak sizzling sounds likened to "mississipiing". The alarm call is a single note, a simple "chick".
DESCRIPTION: Looks like a miniature Red-faced Cisticola or a Neddicky with a spot-tipped tail.

Short-winged Cisticola on calling post

Fan-tailed Flycatcher   *Myioparus plumbeus*
See page 45. A highly active little flycatcher which behaves more like a warbler than the other still-hunting flycatchers.

Sombre Bulbul   *Andropadus importunus*
See page 87.

Yellow-bellied Eremomela   *Eremomela icteropygialis*
See page 52. Goes up into the canopy but not often.

Canopy of thornveld

Thornveld: canopy and mid-level

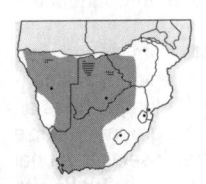

Cape Penduline Tit
Anthoscopus minutus

illustrated page 21
(*Newman's Birds* p. 345)

HABITAT: Thornveld and various other habitats including scrub and coastal bush, mainly in drier areas.
STATUS: Common resident.
BEHAVIOUR: Found in pairs or small parties of 4-10 birds. Joins mixed bird parties. Feeds in the outer canopies of trees, flitting one after another from tree to tree. Constantly on the move.
CALL: Contact call "tritt, tritt".
DESCRIPTION: A tiny bird with diagnostic **black and white speckles** on the forehead. Throat white, breast and belly yellow.

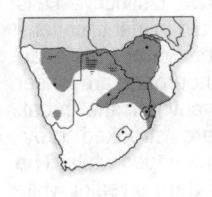

Burnt-necked Eremomela
Eremomela usticollis

illustrated page 22
(*Newman's Birds* p. 345)

HABITAT: Confined to thornveld throughout its range.
STATUS: Common resident.
BEHAVIOUR: A gregarious species found in loose parties of 4-8 birds that follow along in a disjointed, straggling fashion. Joins mixed bird parties where it forages in an active manner. Is noticed mainly by call.
CALL: A very high-pitched rapid piping and trilling that rises and falls as different members of the party fade out and others take over "teeup-ti-ti-ti-ti-ti ...".
DESCRIPTION: Grey above and cream to yellow below. **Only adults have a rusty collar on the throat.**

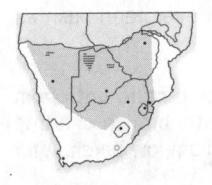

Icterine Warbler
Hippolais icterina

illustrated page 19
(*Newman's Birds* p. 333)

HABITAT: Mainly **thornveld**; also broad-leaved woodland.
STATUS: Fairly common Palaearctic migrant, occurring from mid-October to early April.
BEHAVIOUR: Found in the canopy or mid-level. Restless,

singing with orange mouth wide open. Usually solitary and overlooked when not calling.

CALL: A loud sustained jumble of melodious and jarring notes with high squeaks. Roberts describes the call as a pleasant "dideroit".

DESCRIPTION: Yellowish below. Bill noticeably broad at the base. Shows sloping forehead and pale yellow panel in the folded wing (no panel in wing of Willow Warbler). Legs bluish.

Understorey of broad-leaved woodland

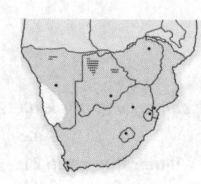

Spotted Flycatcher
Muscicapa striata

illustrated page 28
(*Newman's Birds* p. 363)

HABITAT: Open woodland, wooded parks and gardens, but **prefers drier conditions** than the Dusky Flycatcher.

STATUS: Common non-breeding summer visitor throughout the subregion.

BEHAVIOUR: It **still-hunts** from a shady low perch under the tree canopy but is inconspicuous. It sits quietly for long periods on its perch, then flies to the ground to seize its insect prey, or catches insects in a brief aerial sally. On resettling it **flicks its wings more frequently** than the Dusky Flycatcher.

CALL: Mostly silent but will utter an occasional **sibilant** "zeee" or "zee chick-chick". Unlike many other LBJs, the drab flycatchers do not have distinctive calls that are an important aid in identification.

DESCRIPTION: A drab brown or grey sparrow-sized bird. The underparts are whiter than in the Dusky Flycatcher; the throat, breast and flanks are streaked grey-brown, the wing coverts edged white. **The top of the head has dark streaks** while the head itself sometimes appears peaked.

Spotted or Dusky Flycatcher

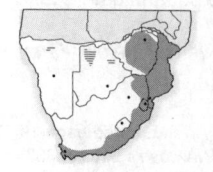

Dusky Flycatcher
Muscicapa adusta

illustrated page 28
(*Newman's Birds* p. 363)

HABITAT: Occurs mostly in the moist eastern regions; frequents lowland and mistbelt evergreen forest fringes, riparian forests, sheltered well-wooded valleys and dense evergreen bush as well as gardens.

STATUS: Common, localised resident.

BEHAVIOUR: Usually seen singly or in pairs. It **still-hunts** from a shady perch on the side of a bush, from a branch of a tree beneath the canopy or from a similar medium-low perch. After catching an insect it often returns to the same perch where it **flicks its wings** after settling.

CALL: It may reveal its presence by its call, a sibilant "tseeee", but is mostly silent.

DESCRIPTION: A small grey-brown flycatcher of **dumpy appearance** and with few distinct markings. Little contrast between the upper- and underparts, but the chin and under-belly are whitish, and there are a few indistinct darker smudges on the upper breast. This resident flycatcher can be confused with the summer-visiting Spotted Flycatcher, but the latter is less dumpy, is not confined to moist regions and has a streaked head.

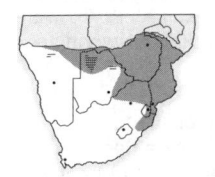

Pallid Flycatcher
Melaenornis pallidus

illustrated page 28
(*Newman's Birds* p. 363)

HABITAT: Broad-leaved woodland with a well-developed understorey, **seldom thornveld**.

STATUS: Common resident.

BEHAVIOUR: Found in pairs or small groups. Still-hunts from a low outer branch on the edge of a clearing, where it flicks its wings occasionally, but is otherwise an unobtrusive bird.

CALL: An occasional thin squeak and an unmusical, rambling song of various scratchy notes.

DESCRIPTION: A plump, monotone grey-brown bird, only slightly paler below. Its **lores are black, eyelids white**: two diagnostic features that can be distinguished at close range. The range of this species does not overlap with that of the similar Chat Flycatcher.

Pallid Flycatcher

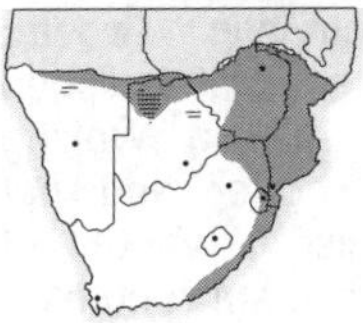

Blue-grey Flycatcher
Muscicapa caerulescens

illustrated page 28
(*Newman's Birds* p. 363)

HABITAT: The mid- and lower strata of riverine forests and broad-leaved woodland.

STATUS: Common resident.

BEHAVIOUR: A quiet and inconspicuous species that perches motionless for long periods on some low branch from where it still-hunts, employing frequent aerial sallies. It often returns to the same perch and flicks its wings on resettling. May also forage on tree trunks, clinging with the body held horizontally.

CALL: The call is characteristic, a strophe of 6-8 soft, sibilant notes of which the first two or three rise and the rest fade, gradually falling in volume and pitch.

DESCRIPTION: In the field appears similar to the Fan-tailed Flycatcher, but shows no white in the tail.

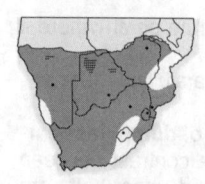

Long-billed Crombec
Sylvietta rufescens

illustrated page 21
(*Newman's Birds* p. 343)

Habitat: Has a very wide distribution, including understorey bush, thickets and surrounding scrub, arid scrub, broad-leaved woodland, thornveld and riverine woodland.
Status: Common resident.
Behaviour: Forages on trunks and into the top branches.
Call: A loud, urgent-sounding "tree-cheer, tree-cheer, tree-cheer ...". Most often heard is the "prrrrp" contact call.
Description: Small, with a very short tail, rufous underparts and a **distinct eye-stripe**.

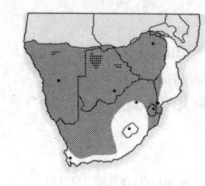

Yellow-bellied Eremomela
Eremomela icteropygialis

illustrated page 22
(*Newman's Birds* p. 345)

Habitat: Low bushes and the edges of thickets in woodland; also the surrounding scrub.
Status: Common resident.
Behaviour: Not found in parties like the penduline tits.
Call: Snatches of 3-4 quick phrases of 6-8 syllables, like the call of the Long-billed Crombec but longer, with 2-3 peaks in each phrase, and not so raspy "chirri-CHEE-CHEE-choo" or "tiree-CHICHI-choo". Also utters a variety of other short compound phrases.
Description: Grey, with yellow only on the belly (the Grey Penduline Tit has a buff belly; the Cape Penduline Tit has a spotted forehead).

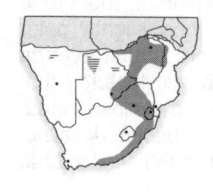

Lazy Cisticola
Cisticola aberrans

illustrated page 24
(*Newman's Birds* p. 357)

Habitat: Found among **rocks**, around the foot of koppies, usually under trees, but also on open granite hillsides with grass and bush.
Status: Common resident.
Behaviour: Runs rapidly over rocks and on the ground. Cocks its tail like a prinia.

Call: Characteristic "wheat, wheat, wheat", short and clipped at the end – like a Wailing Cisticola but shorter and not open-ended. Also a variety of buzzing and jarring **short** notes.
Description: Similar in size to the Rattling Cisticola, but the tail is proportionately longer than that of any other cisticola, and has very faint spotting at the end. Has a rufous crown, but is otherwise plain-looking; no streaking on back.

Lazy Cisticola

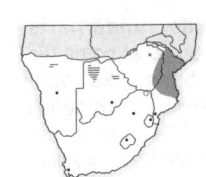

Red-winged Warbler
Heliolais erythroptera

illustrated page 21
(*Newman's Birds* p. 361)

HABITAT: Mozambique and the eastern districts of Zimbabwe in well-developed woodland where there are many scattered bushes, and in tall grass below the woodland canopy.
STATUS: Uncommon resident.
BEHAVIOUR: It behaves like a Tawny-flanked Prinia. Goes about in small parties.
CALL: Utters a pretty twittering call "pseep-pseep-pseep" and goes up into the trees when disturbed. Also makes a high-pitched "chirrr".
DESCRIPTION: The different summer and winter plumages can cause identification problems. In the breeding season (summer) the head and back are a brownish grey. This becomes a rusty colour in winter. **At all times the rufous colouring of the wings is distinctive.**

Neddicky   *Cisticola fulvicapilla*
See page 44.

Short-winged Cisticola   *Cisticola brachyptera*
See page 48.

Stierling's Barred Warbler   *Calamonastes stierlingi*
See page 46. When not calling from a territorial post in the canopy, it forages on the ground in low bushes and at the edge of thickets where it moves around slowly.

Tawny-flanked Prinia   *Prinia subflava*
See page 60. Occurs in almost any habitat within its range.

Tinkling Cisticola   *Cisticola rufilata*
See page 60. Occurs under tree cover on poor soils.

Understorey of thornveld

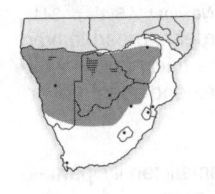

Marico Flycatcher
Melaenornis mariquensis

illustrated page 28
(*Newman's Birds* p. 365)

HABITAT: Thornveld to thorn savanna. Most common in the dry west.
STATUS: Common resident within its range.
BEHAVIOUR: It still-hunts from a low perch **on the side** of a bush. Flies to the ground to seize its insect prey and sometimes forages briefly on the ground, hopping about with its tail raised.
CALL: Its unmusical song, consisting of harsh phrases, is of little help in identification.
DESCRIPTION: **This is the only small still-hunter with highly**

LBJs made easier

Marico Flycatcher still-hunts from side of bush or tree

conspicuous white underparts. Can usually be identified at some distance. Immature birds, like other immatures of the *Melaenornis* genus, are well-spotted white above and blackish below, and are best identified by habitat in the absence of adult birds.

Fan-tailed Flycatcher *Myioparus plumbeus*
See page 45. Can be seen in both woodland types.

Long-billed Crombec *Sylvietta rufescens*
See page 52. Occupies a broad range of habitats with a preference for both types of woodland.

Yellow-bellied Eremomela *Eremomela icteropygialis*
See page 52. In the Karoo, Kalahari and south-western Cape it is most common in thornveld.

Thickets in broad-leaved woodland

Cross-section of a thicket in broad-leaved woodland

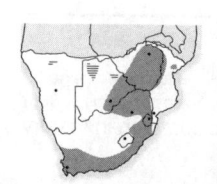

Bar-throated Apalis
Apalis thoracica

illustrated page 20
(*Newman's Birds* p. 341)

HABITAT: A variety of habitats including gardens, broad-leaved woodland, coastal bush, outskirts of riverine thickets and well-wooded kloofs. Also around koppies and extending into evergreen forest edges.

STATUS: Common resident.

BEHAVIOUR: Generally found in pairs or small family parties. Forages mostly in the undergrowth. Joins mixed bird parties. Moves constantly in the thicket interior, but is a rather elusive bird which would often be overlooked were it not for its surprisingly loud and distinctive call.

CALL: Most characteristically a loud, distinctive "pilly-pilly-pilly"

uttered in strophes of 3-4 notes which are repeated after a pause of a few seconds. While one bird calls in this way the mate duets with a short trilled call.
DESCRIPTION: Dark-grey upperparts, white throat, white or yellow breast and a small black collar. There are considerable colour differences between the subspecies. Has **white outer tail feathers.**

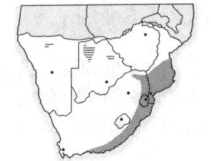

Bleating Warblers
Camaroptera brachyura and *C. brevicaudata*

illustrated page 22

(*Newman's Birds* p. 347)

Green-backed

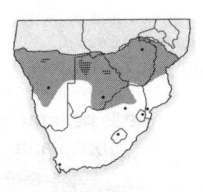

Grey-backed

HABITAT: There are two species, the Green-backed and Grey-backed. The Green-backed Bleating Warbler is found in moist forests in the east of the subregion and the Grey-backed in drier broad-leaved woodland. Occurs from the understorey of evergreen forest at low altitudes to dry deciduous thickets. Common in riverine thickets and on koppies.
STATUS: Common resident.
BEHAVIOUR: Occurs singly or in pairs or small family parties. Feeds low down in the vegetation or on the ground. Gives a striking display: one or two birds bounce up and down to a height of about 30 cm, returning to the perch site as if pulled back by a rubber band. This display is accompanied by an excited call.
CALL: Has a variety of calls; most characteristic is a loud, repetitive double note that sounds like a single note with a distinct zip or snap "e-zit-e-zit-e-zit". Repeated at about 2-3 per second in phrases of 20-30 notes. Also a soft, far-away monosyllabic bleat uttered repetitively, but more slowly or in shorter phrases. This indicates alarm or agitation.
DESCRIPTION: The Green-backed retains its plumage throughout the year. The Grey-backed is brown in winter and grey on the back in summer, but the folded wing always shows plenty of yellow. The tail is short, cocked up over the back.

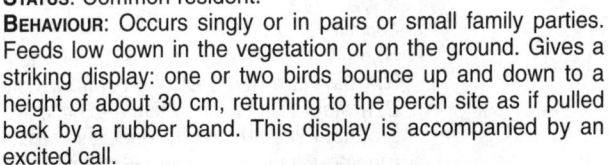

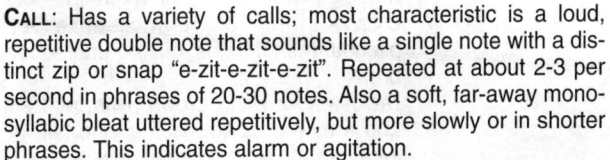

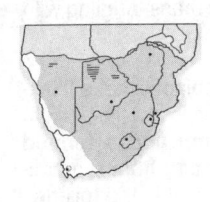

Garden Warbler
Sylvia borin

illustrated page 19

(*Newman's Birds* p. 333)

HABITAT: Dense thickets; also goes into gardens. Has a fairly wide distribution but generally avoids the drier western parts of Namibia and the Cape.
STATUS: Fairly common non-breeding summer visitor, occurring from October to April.
BEHAVIOUR: Occurs singly. Keeps low down inside thickets and stays hidden.
CALL: A protracted soft warbling that can go on and on, uttered from within the cover of the thicket. No harsh noises but frequent pauses.
DESCRIPTION: A plain greyish brown colour. Has no eye-stripe. Face and bill a bit stubby.

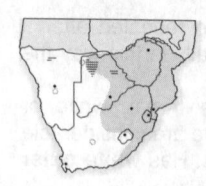

European Marsh Warbler
Acrocephalus palustris

illustrated page 20
(*Newman's Birds* p. 337)

Habitat: Fringes of reed-beds, waterside weeds, **woody thickets** on anthills and leafy vegetation along rivers; also comes into garden hedges.
Status: Common non-breeding summer visitor, occurring from December to April.
Behaviour: Keeps well hidden. A solitary species, generally overlooked unless calling from within the thicket. Seldom still, hopping about just out of vision.
Call: A protracted soft warbling like the Garden Warbler, but **higher-pitched with trills and harsh sounds included**. Uttered from within cover. Also a short, sharp "tuk" repeated at 3-10 second intervals when disturbed.
Description: A plain brown bird. Very similar to the African Marsh Warbler (which is yellow-brown) but more olive above.

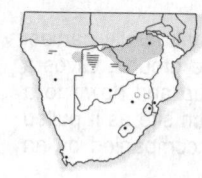

River Warbler
Locustella fluviatilis

illustrated page 19
(*Newman's Birds* p. 335)

Habitat: Dense thickets and reed-beds, mainly in Zimbabwe.
Status: Rare non-breeding summer visitor.
Behaviour: Highly secretive and difficult to find. Feeds near the ground. Flies reluctantly, generally dropping to the ground and running away. Very much a "creep-about" bird.
Call: An **intermittent, cricket-like** "zer-zer-zer-zer ...". High-pitched, monotonous, quickly uttered for 5-10 seconds, then a break.
Description: Plain brown, with faint streaking on the breast and a pale eyebrow. Has a long tail with a rounded end and long, buff-tipped under-tail coverts.

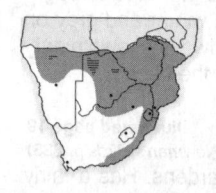

White-browed Scrub Robin
Erythropygia leucophrys

illustrated page 18
(*Newman's Birds* p. 329)

Habitat: Broad-leaved woodland, thornveld and mixed bushveld where thickets are formed by long grass tangling with low bushes, especially on termite hills.
Status: Common resident.
Behaviour: Secretive when not singing, keeping within a thicket or beneath low bushes. If disturbed flies off in low, jerky flight showing its **white wing-bars, orange rump and a fanned black tail** with white feather tips. It sings either from a prominent perch on top of a bush or while concealed in the foliage.
Call: On warm days it sings loudly and for long periods; various phrases are repeated almost without pause "pirit pirit, tertwee tertwee, chee chee, chu-it chu-it ..."; the song phrases differ among individuals.
Description: The white eyebrow is clear, but is a feature shared by some other small brown robins. The **bold streaks on the breast** are diagnostic.

Warblers, robins, etc.

Thickets in thornveld

Cross-section of a thicket in thornveld

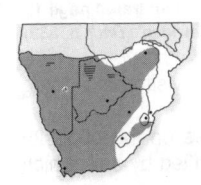

Titbabbler
Parisoma subcaeruleum

illustrated page 20
(*Newman's Birds* p. 343)

HABITAT: Thornveld scrub and thickets; also broad-leaved woodland.
STATUS: Common resident.
BEHAVIOUR: Usually solitary or in pairs, actively searching the thickets and tree canopies for insects and small fruits. Moves with a quick dipping flight from one bush to the next, but seldom goes far.
CALL: Calls frequently, a variety of clear, ringing, quickly rendered notes, typically "cheriktiktik" or "chuu-ti chuu-ti chuu-chuu".
DESCRIPTION: A grey bird with a conspicuous **chestnut vent** – diagnostic. Easy to identify from the illustrations.

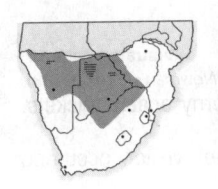

Barred Warbler
Calamonastes fasciolatus

illustrated page 22
(*Newman's Birds* p. 347)

HABITAT: Thornveld in drier regions.
STATUS: Common resident.
BEHAVIOUR: Best located by its call. Found in pairs or small groups and forages well within the thickets, often working its way from the bottom to the top and then flying on to the next bush and repeating the process. Rather deliberate in its movements and quite confiding. The long tail is **cocked up over the back** or fanned, particularly when the bird is agitated.
CALL: A mournful "brreeet-brreeet-brreeet ...", uttered in bursts of 3-5 for long periods.
DESCRIPTION: Breeding birds show a dark breast and barred flanks, whereas non-breeding birds have buff underparts with brown barring.

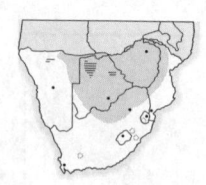

Whitethroat
Sylvia communis

illustrated page 19
(*Newman's Birds* p. 335)

HABITAT: Thornveld thickets and scrub, mainly in the northern parts of the subregion.
STATUS: Uncommon non-breeding summer visitor, occurring from December to April.
BEHAVIOUR: **Always on the move**, darting after insects, raising the crown feathers and fanning the tail.
CALL: A **protracted warbling**, rather scratchy and hurried, and sustained for long periods.
DESCRIPTION: A two-tone bird, the grey-brown upperparts ending below the eye and clearly divided from the white throat. Has white outer tail feathers like an apalis. Eastern races show rufous on the folded wing.

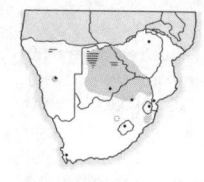

Olive-tree Warbler
Hippolais olivetorum

illustrated page 19
(*Newman's Birds* p. 333)

HABITAT: Mainly dense thorny thickets.
STATUS: Uncommon non-breeding summer visitor, occurring from December to March.
BEHAVIOUR: Found singly. It skulks and stays on the opposite side of the bush to the observer. Best identified by call, which is uttered from within the thicket.
CALL: Louder and deeper than that of most warblers, **a grating jumble of notes with sharp "tch-tch" sounds interspersed**, but slightly more musical than that of the Great Reed Warbler.
DESCRIPTION: Large. Told by the sharply sloping forehead above a white eyebrow, pale edges to the wing feathers plus a two-tone bill, and whitish underparts. Closely resembles the Great Reed Warbler in appearance, but upperparts olive-grey, not brown.

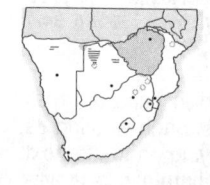

Thrush Nightingale
Luscinia luscinia

illustrated page 19
(*Newman's Birds* p. 333)

HABITAT: Loves *Lantana* thickets; also thorny acacia thickets. Found mainly in Zimbabwe.
STATUS: Uncommon non-breeding summer visitor, occurring mainly from December to March.
BEHAVIOUR: Keeps low down and is usually hidden inside the thicket. Generally solitary and very secretive, but not a "creep-about" bird. More positive than the *Bradypterus* warblers; hops about and comes out to look at you.
CALL: **A protracted, rich mellow** series of chuckling warbles with repeated phrases and a great variety in pitch. Continues calling for a minute or more, pauses briefly and then calls again. Can go on for an hour or so.
DESCRIPTION: A dark brown bird about the size of a Puffback. The breast is faintly speckled. The rump area can seem rufous. Looks and behaves more like a warbler than a small robin.

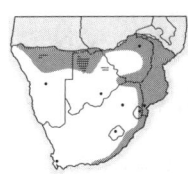

Yellow-breasted Apalis
Apalis flavida

illustrated page 21
(*Newman's Birds* p. 341)

HABITAT: Particularly common in riverine and thornveld thickets at lower altitudes up to about 1 100 m, and at the edges of evergreen forest. Often found in the edges of creeper-covered trees.
STATUS: Common resident.
BEHAVIOUR: A lively little bird, seen mainly in pairs or small groups. If disturbed it may make snapping sounds with the bill and wings. Creeps about in the tangles. It moves slowly but is seldom still for any length of time.
CALL: The normal call is "skee-skee-skee-chi**zz**ick-chi**zz**ick", the latter part with a husky galloping quality. The mate replies "krik-krik-krik". Both calls are quite loud and rather deep for such a little bird.
DESCRIPTION: Smaller than the Bar-throated Apalis, with grey-green head, yellow back and white throat. Breast bright yellow. Male has a black bar in the centre of the breast.

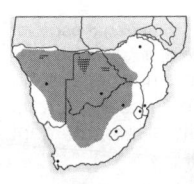

Kalahari Robin
Erythropygia paena

illustrated page 18
(*Newman's Birds* p. 331)

HABITAT: Thornveld, open scrub and old cultivated lands, particularly in arid areas.
STATUS: Common resident.
BEHAVIOUR: Occurs singly or in pairs. Most commonly seen on the ground, where it feeds, often with tail cocked. Runs actively. When alarmed dashes low down into thorn thickets, displaying its characteristic tail pattern. Sings from tree-tops and other perches.
CALL: The high-pitched song is more varied than that of the White-browed Scrub Robin or the Karoo Robin, and repeated regularly "seeoo-seeoo" and "tweetoo-tweetoo, seetoo-seetoo, tritritritri ...". Often perches on a bush calling "twee" intermittently for long periods. The alarm call is a harsh "zeee".
DESCRIPTION: Sandy-brown, with a distinct white eyebrow and a conspicuous rufous tail with black subterminal band and white tips. Much paler, sandier-looking than the Karoo Robin. **Lacks** the white wing-bar and **breast streaks** of the White-browed Scrub Robin, which has rufous on rump only, and a blackish tail with a white tip. Immature Kalahari Robin has lightly spotted underparts.

Terrestrial Bulbul   *Phyllastrephus terrestris*
See page 87. Found in dense thickets in riverine woodland and bushveld, but mainly in forested areas.

White-browed Scrub Robin   *Erythropygia leucophrys*
See page 56. A common resident in thornveld.

GRASSLAND AND MARSHLAND

Fringes of broad-leaved woodland

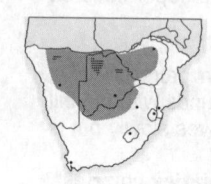

Tinkling Cisticola
Cisticola rufilata

illustrated page 24
(*Newman's Birds* p. 355)

HABITAT: Occurs in drier regions than the Rattling Cisticola, where there is much sparser ground cover with short to very short grass; often associated with Spring Hares.
STATUS: Locally common resident.
BEHAVIOUR: A woodland bird calling from perches but more restrained and less obtrusive than the Rattling Cisticola.
CALL: A loud but **clear** "do-we, do-we, do-we" uttered at a leisurely pace. Alarm is a rapid, clear series of "didididi" notes uttered at the same fairly high pitch.
DESCRIPTION: In appearance similar to the Rattling Cisticola but **very red on top of the head.** The back is well striped.

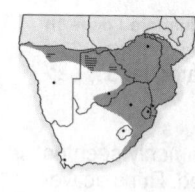

Tawny-flanked Prinia
Prinia subflava

illustrated page 21
(*Newman's Birds* p. 359)

HABITAT: Occurs almost anywhere within its range: in and on the edges of woodland, in forest fringes, open grassland, rank growth in vleis, suburban gardens and even in the emergent vegetation over water on ephemeral pans.
STATUS: Common resident.
BEHAVIOUR: Found in pairs or small family groups. Easily located because of its loud call and conspicuous behaviour, particularly when disturbed. The family groups call constantly from a prominent perch, with tails cocked over the back.
CALL: A quickly uttered "zink-zink-zink", repeated in bouts of 10-40 with a pause before the next call of another 10-40 notes. The alarm call is a plaintive, drawn-out "sbeeeee, sbeeeee".
DESCRIPTION: Can be recognised by its **distinct eyebrow**, its **long thin tail which is often cocked over its back** and by the fact that it often occurs in small family parties of 4-5 birds.

Singing Cisticola
Cisticola cantans

illustrated page 24
(*Newman's Birds* p. 353)

HABITAT: Restricted to the eastern districts of Zimbabwe; found along forest edges in bracken-brier or rank grass and weeds of a softer nature than those preferred by the Red-faced Cisticola.
STATUS: Common resident.
BEHAVIOUR: Found in pairs or small family parties. Generally keeps well hidden within the vegetation, but sometimes comes out to investigate.
CALL: **Does not sing.** Gives a variety of **explosive calls** of two or three syllables – loud, ringing, jarring and with little pat-

tern "jhu-jee" or "wheech-oo". May come out to have a look at you; then calls and protests from exposed positions. Alarm call is repeated like that of a Brier Warbler (Roberts's Prinia): a series of quickly repeated "cheercheercheers", similar in sound to the Rattling Cisticola's opening notes, but uttered in bursts of 10-20 notes and then repeated.
DESCRIPTION: A plain-backed bird with well-spotted tailtip, red on the head and, in winter, the folded wing contrasting with the greyer back.

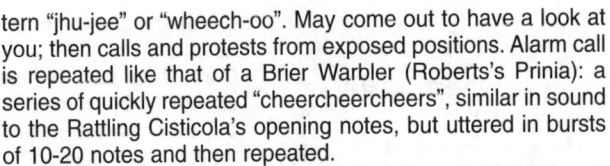

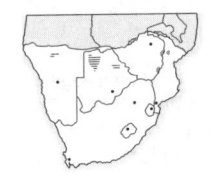

Moustached Warbler
Melocichla mentalis

illustrated page 22
(Newman's Birds p. 349)

HABITAT: Rank grass and scattered bushes on the edge of forests and marshes. Only found in parts of Mozambique and the eastern districts of Zimbabwe, particularly in low-lying areas such as the Honde Valley.
STATUS: Uncommon resident.
BEHAVIOUR: Like the Grassbird, it prefers to skulk within the vegetation, but comes out to the top of the grass or bushes, or even to the middle level of trees, to sing.
CALL: The delightful **warbling song** is "tip-tiptwiddle-iddle-see", the first two sounds slow, the rest fast, the whole strophe lasting 2-3 seconds.
DESCRIPTION: It has **no streaking on the back or breast** (unlike the Grassbird), and is plain reddish brown above with a white throat and breast. There is a clear moustachial streak. Size, shape and jizz more like a tchagra than a warbler.

Grassbird *Sphenoeacus afer*
See page 77.

Neddicky *Cisticola fulvicapilla*
See page 44.

Rattling Cisticola *Cisticola chiniana*
See below. Occurs on the edges of broad-leaved woodland, thornveld and riverine woodland.

---------- **Fringes of thornveld** ----------

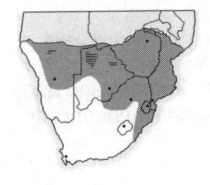

Rattling Cisticola
Cisticola chiniana

illustrated page 23
(Newman's Birds p. 355)

HABITAT: Likes short to long grass and good ground cover. **Must have bushes and elevated perches from which to call.**
STATUS: Common resident.
BEHAVIOUR: A bushveld bird but comes out into the grassland fringes. A noisy species, calling loudly from the top of bushes

LBJs made easier

Rattling Cisticola

or trees; a cheeky, positive bird that demands attention.
CALL: A strident phrase of 4-7 notes introduced by **2-3 harsh "cheers" followed by 3-4 other varied notes.** Alarm is a torrent of "cheer cheer cheers".
DESCRIPTION: Shows few distinctive features, but the back is striped and well patterned at the tailtip. The crown is russet and may be plain or lightly streaked. When calling its black mouth interior is visible.

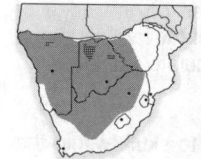

Black-chested Prinia
Prinia flavicans

illustrated page 21
(*Newman's Birds* p. 359)

HABITAT: An arid country species frequenting thornveld in the western parts of the subregion. In some areas enters suburban gardens.
STATUS: Common resident.
BEHAVIOUR/CALL: It joins mixed bird parties and feeds on insects within the bushes. It perches prominently on the top of the vegetation to call, a loud, much-repeated "chip-chip-chip ...". Also utters an occasional "zrrrrt-zrrrrt-zrrrrt". In areas where it overlaps with the Tawny-flanked Prinia it occupies the drier scrub and thickets, with the Tawny-flanked going into the moister vegetation along rivers.
DESCRIPTION: Is often mistaken for a Bar-throated Apalis in areas where this species does not occur; in those areas where the two overlap the Bar-throated Apalis is found in different habitat. In summer breeding dress it is easy to identify: a typical prinia with a black breast-band. In non-breeding birds the breast-band is usually absent and the underparts dull yellow.

Saffron Prinia
Prinia hypoxantha
Also called Spotted Prinia

illustrated page 21
(*Newman's Birds* p. 359)

HABITAT: Mainly moist vegetation at higher altitudes; also along the edge of forests and in rank grass, scrub and bracken.
STATUS: Locally common resident.
BEHAVIOUR/CALL: Very similar to that of the Karoo Prinia.
DESCRIPTION: A **lightly** streaked breast on **saffron-yellow underparts**.

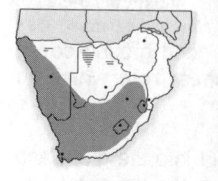

Mountain Chat
Oenanthe monticola

illustrated page 18
(*Newman's Birds* p. 319)

HABITAT: Rocky hills and rock-strewn slopes in grassland and, in some regions, also suburbia; in the arid west it frequents dry riverbeds.
STATUS: Common resident.

BEHAVIOUR: Forages restlessly, often perching on a rock, anthill or fence post. Catches insects on the ground or in brief aerial sallies, then makes off a short distance in low flight.
CALL: An occasional "chit-chit" or a thinly whistled "treeeoop".
DESCRIPTION: Whereas this species is normally identified by the male's striking plumage pattern, a lone female is often perceived as just another LBJ or is mistaken for an Ant-eating Chat. But the female's diagnostic **white vent and outer tail feathers are striking in flight** (the Ant-eating Chat lacks these features).

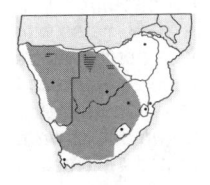

Ant-eating Chat
Myrmecocichla formicivora
illustrated page 18
(*Newman's Birds* p. 323)

HABITAT: Short, dry or overgrazed grassland with scattered rocks, termite mounds and Aardvark burrows.
STATUS: Locally common resident, endemic to South Africa.
BEHAVIOUR: A terrestrial species, perching on rocks, termite mounds, fence posts or small bushes. It makes short hovering flights.
CALL: A thin "peeeck"; the song is an occasional jumble of sustained whistling notes uttered either while perched or in hovering flight.
DESCRIPTION: Appears to be a plain chocolate-brown bird (the male is darker than the female), but when hovering the **primary feathers show as white wing-patches**. Dull white shoulder patches are sometimes present.

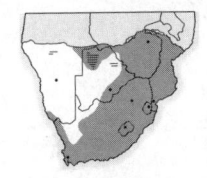

Stonechat
Saxicola torquata
illustrated page 18
(*Newman's Birds* p. 325)

HABITAT: Grassy vleis, fallow lands, scrubland, lush road verges, sugarcane fields and pastures, always near water or in well-irrigated regions.
STATUS: Common resident.
BEHAVIOUR: It perches on some tall weed, fence post, telephone wire or similar vantage point from where it flies to the ground to seize insects. Usually in pairs although not necessarily close together.
CALL: The most frequently heard call is a quiet "seep, TSAK-TSAK" resembling the sound made by two stones being clapped together.
DESCRIPTION: The male is distinctive. While perched the dull brown upperparts and pale cinnamon-coloured underparts of the female are relieved only by the **prominent white wing-patch**. In flight it reveals **white wing-bars and a white rump**.

Open grassland

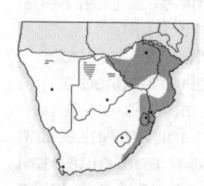

Croaking Cisticola
Cisticola natalensis

illustrated page 24
(*Newman's Birds* p. 357)

HABITAT: A wide variety of grassy conditions from very short to long, but preferably short rank cover. Also grassy patches in otherwise well-wooded areas.

STATUS: Common resident.

BEHAVIOUR: Often perches prominently, particularly during the breeding season.

CALL: Flight call uttered at **about 12 m in low circular cruises**: a loud, rolling "krrRRP" in bouts of about 20-30 notes with little pause. Also a shorter, faster croak. From a perch it utters a drawn-out, rising croak with longer pauses and an **alarm call** likened to "kick-through", a double-note phrase. The agitated female has her own distinctive call, a soft, drawn-out "shwrrrr, shwrrrr" lasting a couple of seconds and repeated 4-6 times at intervals of about 20 seconds.

DESCRIPTION: A large cisticola with a grey crown and streaked back. As big as a female widow, but very white below and has a much longer, slightly curved bill.

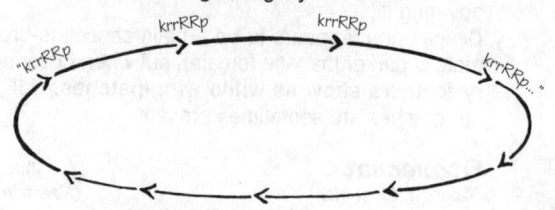

Display flight pattern of Croaking Cisticola

Five almost identical cisticolas
The following five cisticolas are very small and similar in appearance. They all fan their tails, which are notably longer in winter. Best identified during their aerial territorial displays in summer.

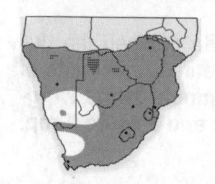

Fan-tailed Cisticola
Cisticola juncidis

illustrated page 23
(*Newman's Birds* p. 351)

HABITAT: A wide variety of grassland types, both wet and dry, but avoids tall grass. In Zimbabwe it occurs all around the shoreline of Lake Kariba on the Torpedo Grass *Panicum repens*. Also in cultivated lands and in semi-arid areas such as along the Orange River, where it would not normally occur, but is now found in irrigated lucerne and other fields.

STATUS: Common and widespread resident, except in the arid western parts of the subregion.

Behaviour/Call: Flight call a very regular "zit-zit-zit", 100 or more at a time, at one-second intervals, while **cruising in wide (200 m) circles at a height of about 50 m** above the ground and **dipping** after each "zit". Alarm call is a rapid "ch-ch-ch-ch-ch" uttered on fluttering wings as it almost hovers about the area of concern. May "zit" from a perch such as overhead power lines and fences. It often dives down over the female at one point of its circular cruise.

Description: Very small. Difficult to recognise by appearance. The back and crown are streaked.

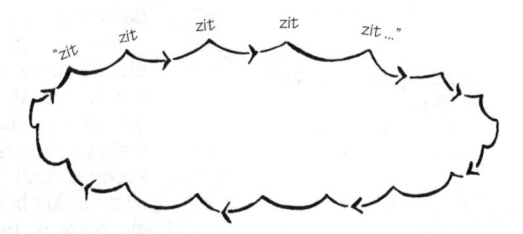

Display flight pattern of Fan-tailed Cisticola

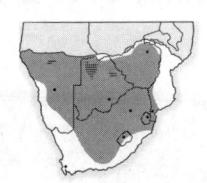

Desert Cisticola
Cisticola aridula

illustrated page 22
(*Newman's Birds* p. 351)

Habitat: Short to long grass; has a preference for patches of unburned grass from the previous season.

Status: Locally common resident, with some movements which are not fully understood.

Behaviour: The display flight takes place at **low altitude** with much climbing and dropping, **wing-snaps** and **irregular dashes** – anything from 5-25 m up. The tail often droops in display flight.

Call: It has two calls: "see see see see" or "zink zink zink zink" uttered in phrases of about 12 notes. The other is "tuk, tuk, tukwee" and combinations of these sounds in short snatches. The two calls are both used in flight. No distinctive alarm call is described.

Description: Small. Nondescript but has a stripy back. In some lights appears paler than the other tail-fanning cisticolas.

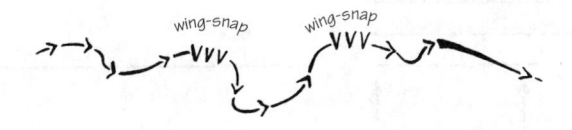

Display flight pattern of Desert Cisticola

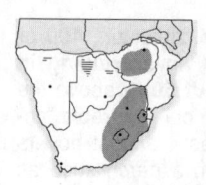

Ayres' Cisticola
Cisticola ayresii

illustrated page 23
(*Newman's Birds* p. 351)

HABITAT: Very short grass on dry ground, including high-altitude grassland in Lesotho and eastern Zimbabwe with bare patches between tufts.

STATUS: Common resident in the eastern half of the subregion.

BEHAVIOUR/CALL: Does not perch in exposed positions and is invisible in the grass as it hides or keeps to the ground. It calls very high up (100-200 m), usually out of sight. **Cruises in an elliptical orbit** calling a deliberate "squeaky squeaky ... lowlow highhigh" as it **flies slowly upwind**. Third and fourth syllables in each phrase are higher than the first two. It does this for 30-40 seconds, and then turns and flies quickly back to the starting point of the orbit with a rapid "tik tik tik tik tik" call before beginning the circuit

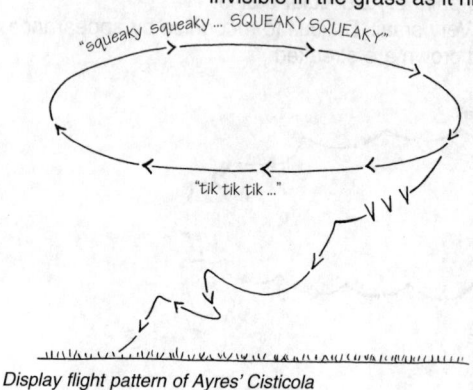

Display flight pattern of Ayres' Cisticola

Grassland Warblers

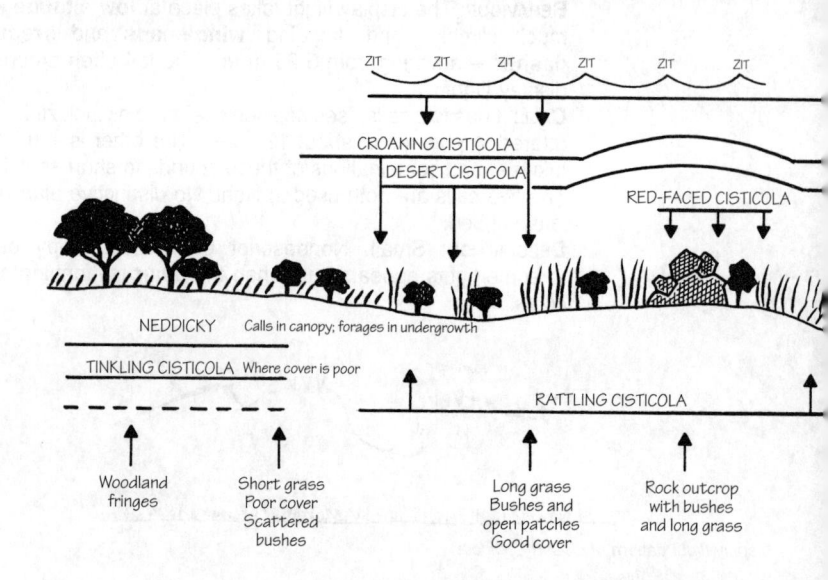

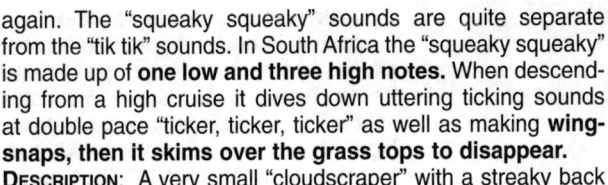

again. The "squeaky squeaky" sounds are quite separate from the "tik tik" sounds. In South Africa the "squeaky squeaky" is made up of **one low and three high notes.** When descending from a high cruise it dives down uttering ticking sounds at double pace "ticker, ticker, ticker" as well as making **wing-snaps, then it skims over the grass tops to disappear.**
DESCRIPTION: A very small "cloudscraper" with a streaky back and short tail.

Pale-crowned Cisticola
Cisticola brunnescens

illustrated page 23
(*Newman's Birds* p. 349)

HABITAT: **Likes short to very short but thickly growing grass** cover at the wetter end of vleis. Often occurs where the ground is **waterlogged** and in short wet grassland below dams. Also in short grass on coastal flats in KwaZulu-Natal.
STATUS: Uncommon resident in most areas, but an altitudinal migrant in KwaZulu-Natal, where it moves from the midland areas to the coastal lowlands during the winter months.
BEHAVIOUR/CALL: The flight call takes place very high up, almost as high as Ayres'; the bird is often invisible. It cruises about more aimlessly than Ayres', uttering a monotonous

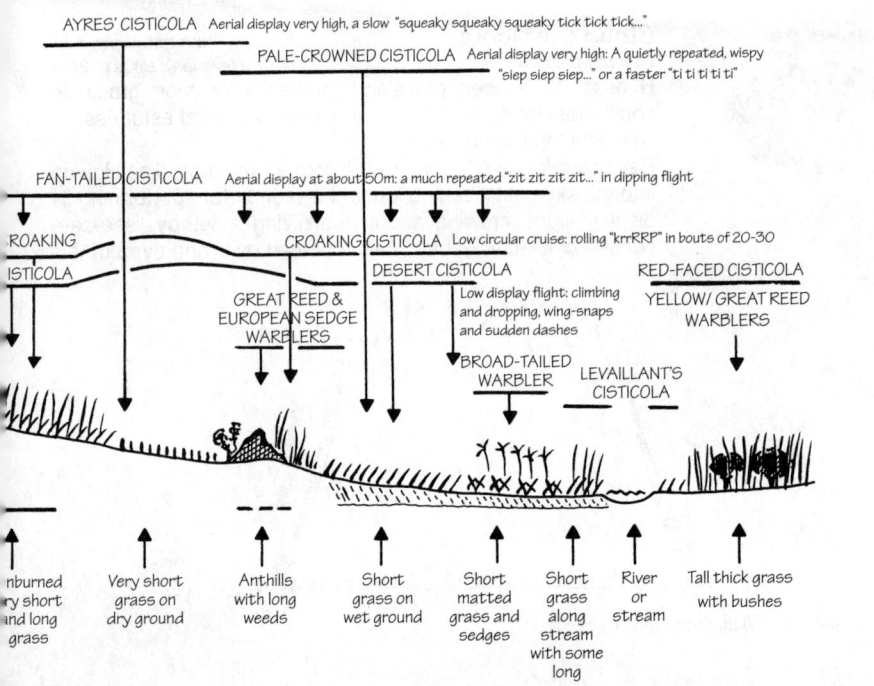

CLOUD CISTICOLA   Aerial display very high, a wispy "see-see-seesee-chick-chick-chick"

AYRES' CISTICOLA   Aerial display very high, a slow "squeaky squeaky squeaky tick tick tick..."

PALE-CROWNED CISTICOLA   Aerial display very high: A quietly repeated, wispy "siep siep siep..." or a faster "ti ti ti ti ti"

FAN-TAILED CISTICOLA   Aerial display at about 50m: a much repeated "zit zit zit zit..." in dipping flight

CROAKING CISTICOLA   Low circular cruise: rolling "krrRRP" in bouts of 20-30

CROAKING CISTICOLA

GREAT REED & EUROPEAN SEDGE WARBLERS

DESERT CISTICOLA   Low display flight: climbing and dropping, wing-snaps and sudden dashes

BROAD-TAILED WARBLER

LEVAILLANT'S CISTICOLA

RED-FACED CISTICOLA

YELLOW/ GREAT REED WARBLERS

Unburned very short and long grass | Very short grass on dry ground | Anthills with long weeds | Short grass on wet ground | Short matted grass and sedges | Short grass along stream with some long | River or stream | Tall thick grass with bushes

LBJs made easier

"squeaky squeaky squeaky squeaky" with a rolling quality and no pauses in bouts of about 20-30 seconds. Males call from exposed perches on longer grass stems: a very high-pitched "tseeu, tseeu, tseeu, tseeu", 5-8 notes getting quicker and softer. This also sometimes precedes bouts of squeaking on high. Alarm call is an explosive whirr of quickly uttered notes that fade away "WHIR-RRR-RRR-rrr-rrr-rrr-rrr".

Display flight pattern of Pale-crowned Cisticola

DESCRIPTION: Like the other "cloudscrapers" it is very small with a short tail. In summer the males have dirty smudges on the face and in front of the shoulder, and the cap is nearly white. It can be readily recognised when sitting on tall grass stems in this plumage.

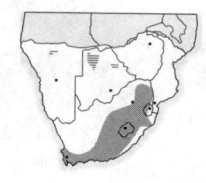

Cloud Cisticola
Cisticola textrix

illustrated page 23
(*Newman's Birds* p. 351)

HABITAT: Very open grassland; prefers very short grass. In south-western Cape it occurs in marshy areas at estuaries.
STATUS: Common resident.
BEHAVIOUR/CALL: A typical "cloudscraper"; the male flies high up into the sky until it can no longer be seen before performing its display flight, cruising about and giving a **wispy** "see-see-seesee-chick-chick-chick" call, repeated over and over. In this

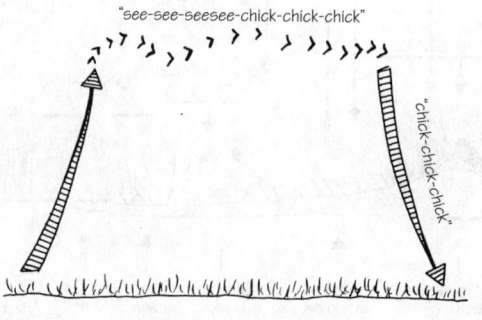

Display flight pattern of Cloud Cisticola

species the "chick chick" follows each "see-see-seesee". It descends back to the grassland in a vertical dive with a rapid "chick-chick-chick-chick" call. **Does not snap its wings.**
DESCRIPTION: Tiny, with a very short tail. In the field indistinguishable from Ayres' Cisticola other than in the southern Cape: the fynbos race is heavily spotted on the breast.

Ant-eating Chat   *Myrmecocichla formicivora*
See page 63. A common inhabitant of short, dry or overgrazed grassland with scattered rocks, termite mounds and burrows.

Mountain Chat   *Oenanthe monticola*
See page 62. The female may cause confusion.

Tawny-flanked Prinia   *Prinia subflava*
See page 60. Found in most habitats; often occurs in tall rank grasses along the edges of cultivation or woodland.

Wailing Cisticola   *Cisticola lais*
See page 75. Found mainly in pairs or small groups in **montane grassland** from the south-western Cape to eastern Zimbabwe, often in patches of scrub, and preferring rocky slopes.

―――― *Marshland* ――――

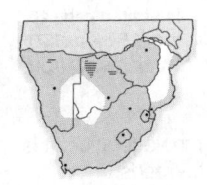

African Marsh Warbler   illustrated page 20
Acrocephalus baeticatus   (*Newman's Birds* p. 337)
HABITAT: Usually found on the outskirts of reed-beds where there is a mixture of grass, sedges, rushes and tall willow herbs. Also occurs away from water, particularly in the Cape.
STATUS: Intra-African migrant breeding in southern Africa in the summer months, widespread throughout. Some birds spend the winter months within the subregion.
BEHAVIOUR: Keeps low in the vegetation where it is difficult to see. One of the few plain-coloured warbling warblers in wet areas.
CALL: A **prolonged warbling**, with much imitation of local birds and harsh notes "chuck chuck weee chirruc churr wurr weee chirruc ...". Continues for a minute or so before pausing, and then carries on after a short break.
DESCRIPTION: Small, and plain brown in colour. The eye-stripe is poorly defined. Very similar to the European Reed Warbler *Acrocephalus scirpaceus*, and the two are almost impossible to distinguish in the field, even by experts. The calls, too, are virtually identical. As the European Reed Warbler is rare in southern Africa, it has not been included in this book.

Marshland Warblers

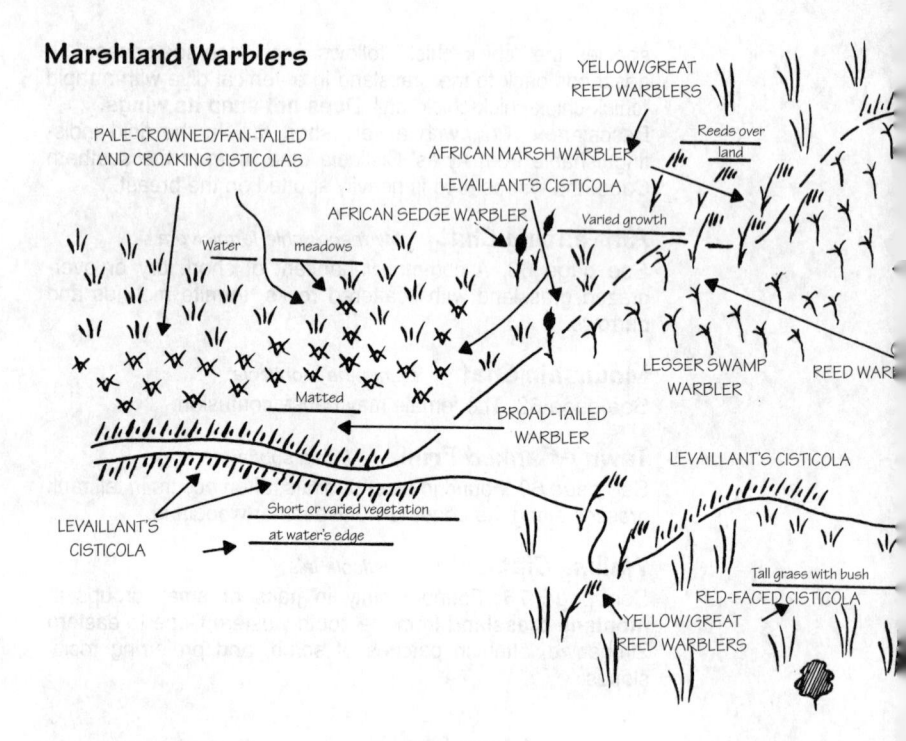

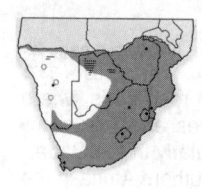

Diagram showing habitat zones with labels:
- PALE-CROWNED/FAN-TAILED AND CROAKING CISTICOLAS
- YELLOW/GREAT REED WARBLERS
- AFRICAN MARSH WARBLER
- LEVAILLANT'S CISTICOLA
- AFRICAN SEDGE WARBLER
- Reeds over land
- Water
- meadows
- Varied growth
- Matted
- LESSER SWAMP WARBLER
- REED WARB[LER]
- BROAD-TAILED WARBLER
- LEVAILLANT'S CISTICOLA
- Short or varied vegetation at water's edge
- LEVAILLANT'S CISTICOLA
- Tall grass with bush
- RED-FACED CISTICOLA
- YELLOW/GREAT REED WARBLERS

Cape Reed Warbler
Acrocephalus gracilirostris

illustrated page 20
(*Newman's Birds* p. 337)

HABITAT: Prefers *Phragmites* and is never found away from water; usually **over water**.
STATUS: Common resident.
BEHAVIOUR: Although it forages low down in the vegetation, it is inquisitive and comes readily to the top of the reeds.
CALL: Short, loud phrases of rich mellow notes "chiroo chiroo tiririiri" punctuated by well-defined pauses.
DESCRIPTION: A slender-billed reed warbler, plain brown above, off-white below, with a **distinct eye-stripe**. The grey legs are obvious.

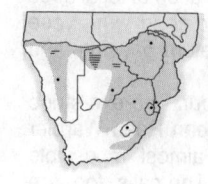

Great Reed Warbler
Acrocephalus arundinaceus

illustrated page 19
(*Newman's Birds* p. 339)

HABITAT: Found in *Phragmites* and tall grass; also on anthill islands with tall grass and into open grassland and surrounding suburban hedges and thickets.
STATUS: Fairly common non-breeding summer visitor, occurring from December to March or April.
BEHAVIOUR/CALL: Call is a distinctive series of **protracted**

Warblers, robins, etc.

Habitat diagram labels:

- LEVAILLANT'S CISTICOLA
- Bushes
- EUROPEAN SEDGE WARBLER
- AFRICAN SEDGE WARBLER
- Bulrushes
- AFRICAN MARSH WARBLER
- Dam wall
- Reeds over water
- [AF]RICAN MARSH WARBLER — Lower levels
- Varied
- LEVAILLANT'S
- Water meadows
- YELLOW & GREAT REED WARBLER
- BROAD-TAILED WARBLER
- PALE-CROWNED CISTICOLA

Symbol	Vegetation
／	REEDS (Phragmites)
／	BULRUSH (Typha)
＼|／	TALL GRASS (Hyparrhenia)
⚘	WILLOW HERD (Epilobium)
Y	RUSHES & SEDGES (Juncus, Cyperus, Scirpus)
××	SHORT MATTED GRASS
＼|／	WATER MEADOWS SHORT GRASS (Leersia)
|/|/|	WATER'S EDGE SHORT & VARIED VEGETATION

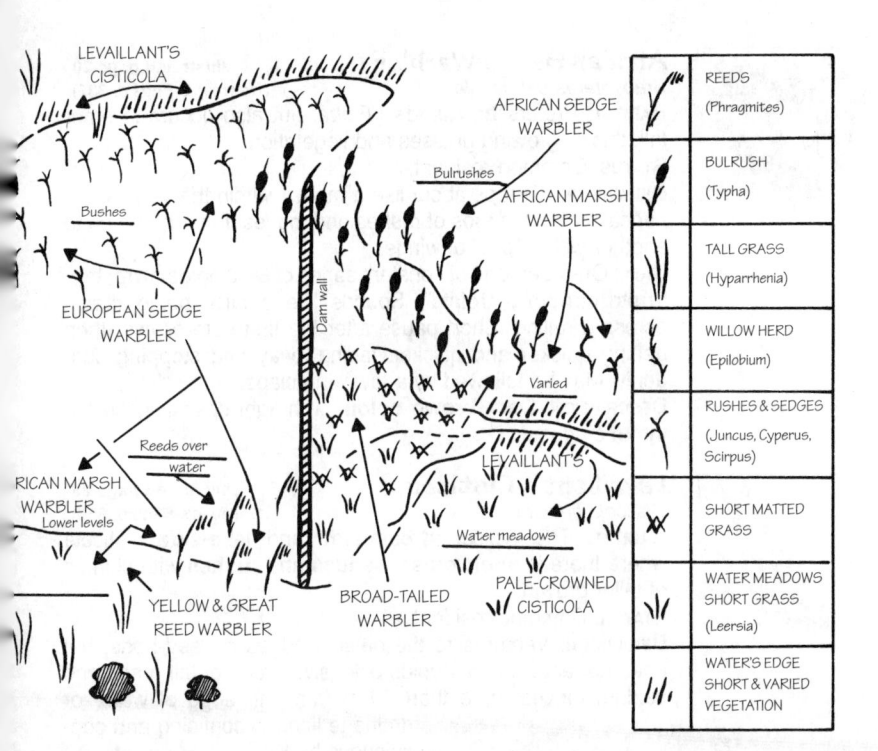

harsh crackles, grates and squawks; loud and quite unmusical. Occurs singly, sometimes in pairs; seldom more.
DESCRIPTION: A large warbler, the size of a weaver but longer in body. Plain brown in colour and looks rather pale as it flies quickly from one clump of cover to another.

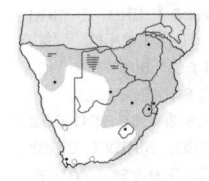

European Sedge Warbler   illustrated page 20
Acrocephalus schoenobaenus   (*Newman's Birds* p. 337)

HABITAT: Found in reed-beds and long grass, but more often in low-growing rush beds. Also grassland anthills, usually close to water. Likes sewage farms.
STATUS: Common non-breeding summer visitor, occurring mainly from December to April or May.
BEHAVIOUR: Not as shy as the other reed or marsh warblers, and comes out to look at you. Often occurs in large numbers.
CALL: A prolonged warbling like the other European migrants but also has single "bzzz" plus "tk" notes – the whole reed-bed may be alive with "bzzz" sounds.
DESCRIPTION: The very distinct eyebrow plus striped crown and back are diagnostic.

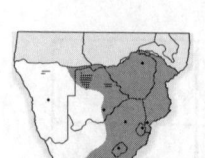

African Sedge Warbler
Bradypterus baboecala   (*Newman's Birds* p. 337)

illustrated page 20

HABITAT: Prefers **bulrushes** (*Typha*) but also occurs in other tall, thickly growing grasses and vegetation.

STATUS: Common resident.

BEHAVIOUR: Creeps about like a mouse within the vegetation, but calls from the tops of rushes and moves from one perch to another with a "prrr" of wings.

CALL: Oft-repeated but constant series of 8-10 notes "trrrp, trrp, trrrptrrrptrrrptrrrp trptptp". Sounds like a stick being drawn across a railing. Short pause after the first note or two, then getting quicker and quicker, fading away and stopping suddenly. May be followed by a few wing-claps.

DESCRIPTION: **Dark brown colour** with light speckling on the throat diagnostic.

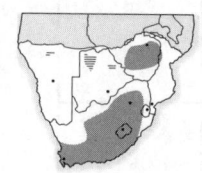

Levaillant's Cisticola
Cisticola tinniens   (*Newman's Birds* p. 355)

illustrated page 23

HABITAT: The typical **stream-side** and **lake-side** cisticola where there is **short grass, sedges and rushes** with clumps of taller growth.

STATUS: Common resident.

BEHAVIOUR: Ventures to the outside edges of reed-beds, but does not enter them. Avoids extensive areas of tall grass and seldom moves more than 30 m from the edge of water or drainage lines. A confiding and conspicuous bird.

CALL: The call is a **whistled song** of 5-8 quickly uttered syllables that fall in tone and then rise at the end "tseep, tseep, tsittorooree". Pretty but not far-carrying. Alarm call is a series of persistent plaintive "dzwee, dzwee, dzwee" notes uttered at about two per second, and continuing for bouts of 10-20 calls, often given in low bouncy flight. A new bout starts after a short pause.

DESCRIPTION: It has a **rich red cap**, the back is striped, almost black, and the underparts are **very white**.

Typical habitat of Levaillant's Cisticola

Red-faced Cisticola
Cisticola erythrops   (*Newman's Birds* p. 357)

illustrated page 24

HABITAT: Common in **long grass and tall, rank reeds** along rivers and streams, and on edges of marshes where there are **bushes**. Also in the shrub layer of open riverine forest, and away from water where such conditions occur.

STATUS: Locally common resident, restricted to the north-east.

BEHAVIOUR: An elusive species which skulks in the rank undergrowth and is difficult to see, except when the male flies up to an exposed perch to sing.
CALL: Song is a loud clear call of 6-10 notes, the first 2-4 rising quickly and the rest descending slowly but markedly "ti ti ti TEE TEE TEE TEE tee tee", the final five phases deliberate and descending, likened to "upUPUPDOWN, DOWN, down ... down". It pauses and then repeats the call. Also calls a loud, even "trree trree trree trree". Alarm call a weak wailing series of "peeoos" like a Tawny-flanked Prinia but thinner.
DESCRIPTION: Very plain (no streaking on the back or crown), with a slightly rufous face and well-marked tailtip.

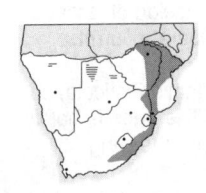

Yellow Warbler
Chloropeta natalensis

illustrated page 20
(*Newman's Birds* p. 339)

HABITAT: Eastern parts of the subregion in *Phragmites* and tall grass. Often away from water. Occurs in bracken-brier and rough growth on hillsides; also on edge of evergreen forest.
STATUS: Fairly common resident; an altitudinal migrant in KwaZulu-Natal.
BEHAVIOUR: Generally solitary or in pairs. Feeds low down where it creeps through the vegetation. Sings from the top of a bush, but disappears into the vegetation when disturbed.
CALL: Rather like the Cape Reed Warbler, but not as mellow, and phrases a bit more protracted "trrp-trrp-chirichirichirichiri".
DESCRIPTION: Olive-brown upperparts and clear yellow underparts are distinctive.

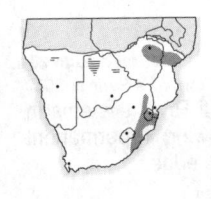

Broad-tailed Warbler
Schoenicola brevirostris

illustrated page 19
(*Newman's Birds* p. 335)

HABITAT: Likes short matted grass with the odd tall clump of sedge from which to call. Also occurs on the fringes of swamps. In the eastern districts of Zimbabwe also in low matted tangles of grass and bracken-brier on open hillsides, not necessarily near water.
STATUS: Uncommon resident in low-lying coastal areas and Mozambique. A summer visitor to high altitudes, including Zimbabwe.
BEHAVIOUR: Found singly or in pairs. Well hidden for most of the day in the vegetation, where it creeps about like a mouse and can be difficult to flush. Most commonly seen in early mornings and evenings, when it perches on top of grasses or bushes. Performs short aerial cruises with tail held down, as though heavy.
CALL: Males have a weak metallic "trreep, trreep, trreep" call, females a harsh "chick" and "zink, zink, zink" repeated rapidly and frequently.
DESCRIPTION: The large dark tail plus small head and bill are distinctive.

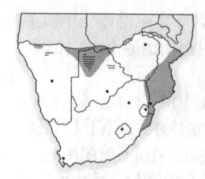

Black-backed Cisticola
Cisticola galactotes

illustrated page 23
(Newman's Birds p. 355)

HABITAT: Tall grasses, sedges and reeds at the edge of lakes, rivers and lagoons. Not always over water. In KwaZulu-Natal it can be found in sugarcane fields.
STATUS: Fairly common resident; common in the Okavango Delta.
BEHAVIOUR: Skulks low down in the vegetation, but during the breeding season the males are very conspicuous, calling loudly from the top of the vegetation. Performs a slow display flight over the reed-beds.
CALL: The rasping or "winding" call, which gives rise to its alternative name – Winding Cisticola – is a succession of "zreeee" or "rraaaare" notes. Also calls a loud, deliberate "prrrit prrrit prrrit prrrit".
DESCRIPTION: Similar in appearance to Levaillant's Cisticola, but the two species scarcely overlap in range. The back is boldly streaked black and it shows a rufous patch on the wing.

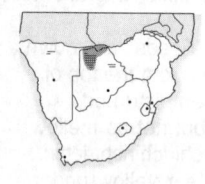

Greater Swamp Warbler
Acrocephalus rufescens

illustrated page 20
(Newman's Birds p. 339)

HABITAT: Limited distribution; occurs in papyrus swamps.
STATUS: Locally common resident.
BEHAVIOUR/CALL: Large but secretive. Not easily seen, but easily located by its loud, short song with guttural notes "churr-churr, chirrup, chuckle", shivering its tail while singing. Also utters an occasional "churr" or "chirr-up" sound.
DESCRIPTION: Dark, with **no eye-stripe.**

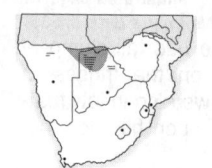

Chirping Cisticola
Cisticola pipiens

illustrated page 23
(Newman's Birds p. 353)

HABITAT: Mainly the Okavango and Linyanti River systems in Botswana. Prefers papyrus and reeds growing in permanent water. Seldom found away from the water's edge.
STATUS: Common resident.
BEHAVIOUR: In the breeding season the male performs a characteristic display flight low over the vegetation with its tail fanned and flicked from side to side as if loose; otherwise keeps well within the vegetation.
CALL: The song is four twanging notes "trrrit-trrrit-trree-treeeeeee". There is a distinct pause after the first note, the next two follow in quick succession and then the long, drawn-out "treeeeeee".
DESCRIPTION: The back is stripy but not as heavily streaked as that of the Black-backed or Levaillant's Cisticola.

Display flight pattern over papyrus or reeds

European Marsh Warbler   *Acrocephalus palustris*
See page 56. More often than not seen **away from the water's edge in woody thickets on anthills, and in garden hedges.** It does however occur on the fringes of reed-beds and in waterside weeds.

Tawny-flanked Prinia   *Prinia subflava*
See page 60. Occurs in most habitats; common in reeds and sedges in vleis.

Rocky hillsides

Mountain Chat   *Oenanthe monticola*
See page 62. The female may cause confusion.

FYNBOS

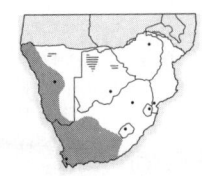

Grey-backed Cisticola   illustrated page 23
Cisticola subruficapilla   (*Newman's Birds* p. 353)
HABITAT: A variety of habitats ranging from fynbos to grassland around estuaries, Karoo scrub and grassy foothills in the north-eastern Cape and Namibia.
STATUS: Common resident.
BEHAVIOUR: It generally feeds low down in the vegetation, but perches high up in the open from where it calls "prouee, tweep, tweep".
CALL: The song, given during the breeding season only, is a hurried high-pitched jumble of descending notes "weesisee-chizzarizzaree-chichioo ...". The alarm note is a piping "tee-tee-tee".
DESCRIPTION: Very similar to the Wailing Cisticola but has **greyish underparts** instead of buffy underparts. In areas where both species occur they can be separated by habitat: the Wailing prefers rocky hillsides with long grass and scattered shrubs, the Grey-backed favours more open scrubby vegetation and flatter areas. Grey-backed Cisticolas in the south-western Cape are spotted on the breast.

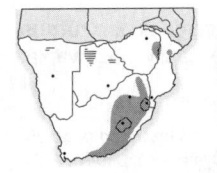

Wailing Cisticola   illustrated page 24
Cisticola lais   (*Newman's Birds* p. 355)
HABITAT: **Montane grassland** from the south-western Cape to eastern Zimbabwe, often in patches of scrub, and preferring rocky slopes.
STATUS: Common resident.
BEHAVIOUR: Found mainly in pairs or small groups. Often sits on rocks, anthills and low bushes, and calls from exposed positions.

CALL: Often a characteristic single note, a little protracted and fading, not clipped short: "wheeee", repeated at well-spaced intervals. Sometimes a three-note "trrrrweeee-twee-twee". Also has a variety of other short notes never strung together.
DESCRIPTION: Very similar to the Rattling, Lazy and Grey-backed Cisticolas. Unlikely to occur alongside the Rattling Cisticola, and differs from the Grey-backed in **habitat preference and buff belly and flanks** (Grey-backed has greyish underparts). The Lazy Cisticola is only faintly streaked on the back. The tail of the Wailing Cisticola looks gingery as the bird flies away.

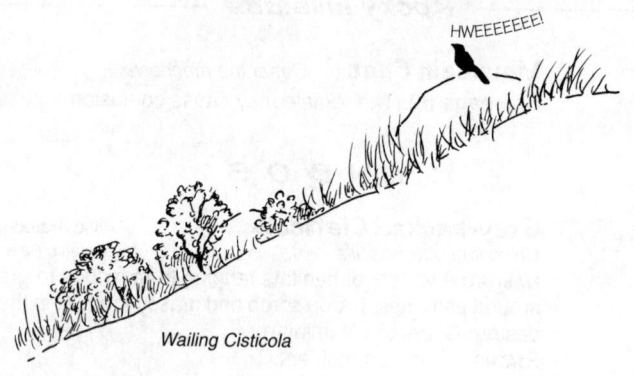

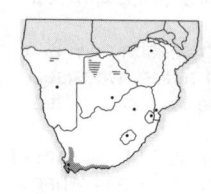

Wailing Cisticola

Victorin's Warbler
Bradypterus victorini

illustrated page 19
(*Newman's Birds* p. 335)

HABITAT: Restricted to mountainous areas from the south-western Cape to Port Elizabeth, where it lives in dense montane scrub, rocky kloofs and the vegetation along mountain streams.
STATUS: Fairly common localised resident, endemic to the winter-rainfall region.
BEHAVIOUR: Usually seen singly. Feeds low down in thick vegetation or even on the ground. Although very secretive it does come out to sing from the top of a low bush or rock.
CALL: In the brief song the notes go up and down with increasing rapidity "mississipippippi".
DESCRIPTION: When singing from an exposed perch the **rufous underparts and orange-yellow eye** are easily observable: diagnostic.

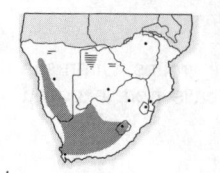

Layard's Titbabbler
Parisoma layardi

illustrated page 20
(*Newman's Birds* p. 343)

HABITAT: Karoo, rocky mountain slopes, fynbos, montane and coastal scrub in the south and dry west.
STATUS: Uncommon resident.

BEHAVIOUR: Creeps about actively within cover, then darts to the next bush with quick, jerky flight.
CALL: Has several clear song phrases, each interspersed with rattling notes "chiroo-chiroo-chiroo, trrrr, chiree-chiree-chiree-trrrr...".
DESCRIPTION: **White (not chestnut) vent**, unlike the Titbabbler.

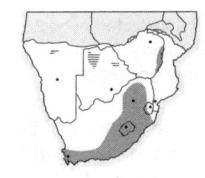

Grassbird
Sphenoeacus afer

illustrated page 22
(*Newman's Birds* p. 349)

HABITAT: Fynbos in the Cape and rank grassland with scattered bushes further north, particularly on mountain slopes and in river valleys; also forest edges. In eastern Zimbabwe it is confined to areas above 1 500 m, where it frequents brackenbrier, bushes and small patches of open coarse grass.
STATUS: Common endemic resident, fairly widespread in southern Africa.
BEHAVIOUR: Generally hides in the vegetation, but perches conspicuously when sunning itself or singing.
CALL: Utters pretty cascading phrases of notes ending in a longer trill or whistle lasting about two seconds, and repeated every 5-10 seconds "chirp-chirp-chirp-does it tickle yoooou". Also gives a cat-like mewing.
DESCRIPTION: Large; bulbul-sized. Has **moustachial streaks and pointed or frayed ends to the thin tail.** The heavily streaked back prevents confusion with the Moustached Warbler.

Karoo Prinia   *Prinia maculosa*
See page 80. This typical prinia is common in coastal fynbos.

Neddicky   *Cisticola fulvicapilla*
See page 44. Resident in montane fynbos in the southwestern Cape where it forages in the undergrowth, but calls from the top of the vegetation.

KAROO AND SEMI-ARID AREAS
(This habitat includes grassy, rock-strewn hillsides and semi-arid grassland.)

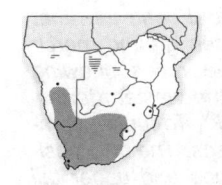

Karoo Robin
Erythropygia coryphaeus

illustrated page 18
(*Newman's Birds* p. 331)

HABITAT: Karoo scrub, thorny riverine scrub and hillsides in the semi-arid southern and western regions.
STATUS: Common endemic resident.
BEHAVIOUR: A conspicuous, inquisitive and noisy bird. If disturbed it perches in full view and calls loudly while flicking its tail. It feeds on the ground and in the lower vegetation.
CALL: A scratchy "chip chip shweet shweety tweety tweety ... ";

the song is a series of unmusical choppy single-syllable notes interspersed with harsh "trrrr" sounds.
DESCRIPTION: This otherwise dull robin has bold white eyebrows and a **white throat with black moustachial streaks**. The black tail is **tipped white**, prominent when fanned as in display or flight.

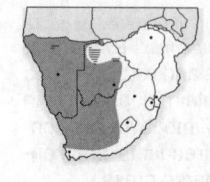

Chat Flycatcher
Melaenornis infuscatus

illustrated page 28
(*Newman's Birds* p. 365)

HABITAT: Thorn scrub and thorn savanna in the dry west.
STATUS: Common resident.
BEHAVIOUR: A conspicuous roadside bird in some areas. It still-hunts from the top of a bush, fence or telephone wire and drops to the ground for its prey, which is eaten either there or on a perch. **While on the ground it holds its wings partially spread**.
CALL: Not very vocal but does utter various chirruping and chirping sounds, nothing distinctive.
DESCRIPTION: Drab appearance. Larger and plumper than the similar Pallid Flycatcher, but their ranges do not overlap. Immature birds are spotted white above and dark below.

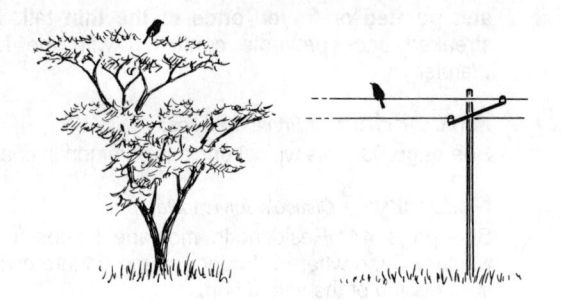

Favoured perches of the Chat Flycatcher

Chats of the genus *Cercomela*
The following four species are so similar in appearance and behaviour that they create many identification problems. All frequent open ground, perch conspicuously and habitually flick their wings. All have races showing plumage variations: darkest in the eastern and palest in the western forms, with graduations between the extremes. All call "chak chak". To further compound the problem all four species have distribution overlaps. The only positive field identification is the colour patterns of their rumps and upper tail coverts. The immatures are all spotted buff above and scaled dark brown below; they do, however, show the same tail patterns as the adults.

Warblers, robins, etc.

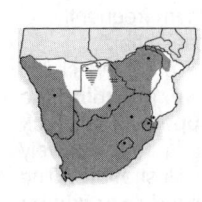

Chat tails and typical posture

Familiar Chat
Cercomela familiaris

illustrated page 18
(*Newman's Birds* p. 321)

HABITAT: Rocky ground, often in hilly country, stone walls, farmyards and dry dongas throughout the subregion with the exception of most of Botswana.

STATUS: Common resident.

BEHAVIOUR: A tame and confiding species. **Flicks its wings several times after settling and after most other movements; it also quivers its tail.**

CALL: Identical to other *Cercomela* chats: "chak chak".

DESCRIPTION: This is the darkest of the four *Cercomela* chats, being dull brown above with darker flight feathers indistinctly edged paler. It has rufous ear coverts (not a good field character) and the underparts are only slightly paler than the upperparts. The western or Namib race is paler in all respects but can still be told from the Namib race of the Karoo Chat by rump and tail patterns. The **rump and tail are chestnut-brown**, the central feathers and subterminal band black, this **forming an inverted T-shape**; see illustrations.

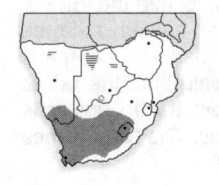

Sickle-winged Chat
Cercomela sinuata

illustrated page 18
(*Newman's Birds* p. 321)

HABITAT: Karoo, short scrubby vegetation in semi-desert, rocky mountain grassland and fallow croplands.

STATUS: Locally common resident, endemic to South Africa.

BEHAVIOUR: It perches on low bushes and fences, dropping to the ground to feed where it stands with upright posture, appearing comparatively long-legged. Flicks its wings less obviously than the similar Familiar Chat, spends more time on the ground and runs more quickly.

CALL: Identical to other *Cercomela* chats: "chak chak".

DESCRIPTION: Differs from the Familiar Chat in that the grey-brown upperparts **contrast** with the paler underparts (there is

LBJs made easier

little difference between upper- and underparts in the Familiar Chat); folded wing shows paler feather edges and the whitish eye-rings are more prominent. The **rump grades to pale chestnut or dull straw-yellow**, the tail feathers are blackish with pale chestnut on their outer vanes: full length on the outermost feathers and progressively less on the adjoining ones, so **forming a distinct dark triangle or wedge shape** (not an inverted T-shape as in the Familiar Chat); see illustrations.

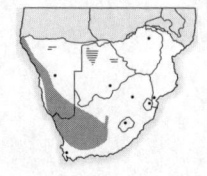

Karoo Chat
Cercomela schlegelii

illustrated page 18
(*Newman's Birds* p. 321)

HABITAT: Scrubby and bushy terrain and rocky hillsides in the Karoo.
STATUS: Common resident, endemic to South Africa.
BEHAVIOUR: It perches on telephone wires, bushes and fences. It **flutters its wings on settling** and flicks them frequently.
CALL: Identical to other *Cercomela* chats: "chak chak".
DESCRIPTION: This is the largest of the four *Cercomela* chats. The south-eastern race is **mainly grey above, including the rump**; only the under-belly is paler. **The upper tail is black with all-white outer feathers**, and the tail is comparatively longer than that of the Tractrac Chat; see illustrations. The smaller Namib race is pale buff in colour with **darker wings; the rump is white**.

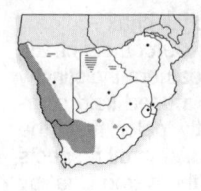

Tractrac Chat
Cercomela tractrac

illustrated page 18
(*Newman's Birds* p. 321)

HABITAT: Flat, arid grassland, Karoo and desert scrub, and gravel plains.
STATUS: Fairly common endemic resident.
Behaviour: It perches on low shrubs or stones but forages on the ground where it runs swiftly. It flicks its wings and jerks its tail frequently.
CALL: Identical to other *Cercomela* chats: "chak chak".
DESCRIPTION: This is the smallest and plumpest of the four *Cercomela* chats; paler and greyer than either the Sickle-winged or Familiar Chat. In the dark south-eastern race the upperparts are ashy-brown, the wings darker, underparts whitish. The rump is white, off-white or pale buff, the **tail is white with a solid triangle of black from its tip upwards towards the central apex**; see illustrations. The **Namib race is nearly white** with darker wings and tail.

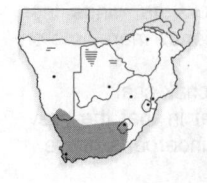

Karoo Prinia
Prinia maculosa

illustrated page 21
(*Newman's Birds* p. 359)

HABITAT: Karoo and montane scrub, coastal fynbos, rank grass along streams and cultivated lands; also exotic plantations. It prefers thick cover 1-2 m in height.
STATUS: Common resident.

BEHAVIOUR: Generally found in pairs or small family parties. Feeds well within the cover, coming to the top of the vegetation when disturbed.
CALL: A chirping "tweet-tweet-tweet ...". Also gives a churring alarm note.
DESCRIPTION: The **underparts are well streaked or spotted**. The tail is long and often cocked over the back in typical prinia fashion.

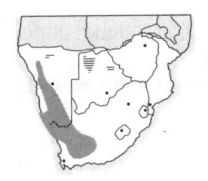

Karoo Eremomela
Eremomela gregalis

illustrated page 22
(*Newman's Birds* p. 347)

HABITAT: Karoo scrub, especially the low scrubby vegetation along drainage lines or watercourses.
STATUS: Uncommon endemic resident.
BEHAVIOUR: Occurs in pairs or small groups. Feeds on the ground and in the scrubby bushes.
CALL: Generally sings before sunrise: a high-pitched "peewip, peewip ..." repeated over and over for up to two minutes at a time. The contact call within the group is a sharp "twinck".
DESCRIPTION: Could be mistaken for a Bleating Warbler, but their ranges do not overlap. Has pale yellow eyes (Bleating Warbler has dark eyes) and pale yellow under-tail coverts.

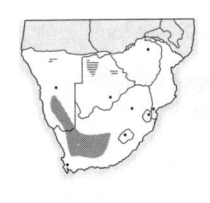

Cinnamon-breasted Warbler
Euryptila subcinnamomea

illustrated page 22
(*Newman's Birds* p. 347)

HABITAT: Hillsides strewn with rocks or bushes in the arid west.
STATUS: Uncommon endemic resident.
BEHAVIOUR: An unobtrusive species which feeds quietly among the rocks and is easily overlooked. It is nevertheless very agile, hopping from rock to rock, flicking its tail up and down. The call, given from the summit of a hill or rocky outcrop, is the best way to locate this elusive bird.
CALL: A plaintive whistle "eeeeeee" lasting about 1,5 seconds.
DESCRIPTION: Despite the bird's name, its cinnamon breast is not easy to see unless close up, but the **dark tail, frequently cocked** up in the air, is diagnostic.

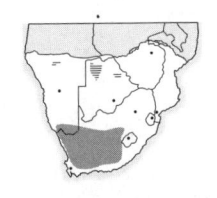

Namaqua Warbler
Phragmacia substriata

illustrated page 21
(*Newman's Birds* p. 359)

HABITAT: Thorny scrub and reed-beds along rivers and near dams in the Karoo; also gardens in parts of its range.
STATUS: Fairly common resident, endemic to the Karoo.
BEHAVIOUR: Occurs in pairs or small family groups. A secretive but active species, feeding well within the vegetation.
CALL: An explosive "tchit-churr". It also utters "che-kee-kee". The song is a rapid series of "tik-tik-tik-tik ..." notes.
DESCRIPTION: Can be confused with the Karoo Prinia but has **white underparts which are lightly streaked** (Karoo Prinia has yellowish underparts) and the flanks and vent are rufous.

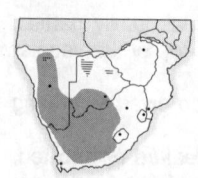

Rufous-eared Warbler
Malcorus pectoralis

illustrated page 21
(*Newman's Birds* p. 361)

HABITAT: Low scrubby Karoid vegetation, including scrubby hillsides, in the arid west.
STATUS: Fairly common resident.
BEHAVIOUR: Spends quite a bit of time **feeding on the ground**, hopping actively between bushes, preferring to run rather than fly, and holding its long, thin tail upright or cocked over its back like a prinia.
CALL: Males call from the top of the vegetation, a loud, penetrating "tee, tee, tee, tee" plus a quiet "chit".
DESCRIPTION: The **black breast-band** and **rufous ear coverts** are diagnostic.

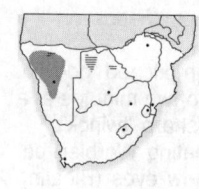

Rockrunner
Achaetops pycnopygius
Also called Damara Rockjumper

illustrated page 22
(*Newman's Birds* p. 349)

HABITAT: Confined to grassy, rocky hillsides and dry watercourses in Namibia.
STATUS: Common resident but rather elusive; endemic to Namibia.
BEHAVIOUR: It calls from a prominent perch such as a rock or bush, particularly in the early morning and evening.
CALL: The song is a warbling "tip-tip-tootle-tootle-too". It also mimics the calls of other birds.
DESCRIPTION: Heavily streaked on the back; shows a white throat and breast, as well as bold facial markings.

Cape Penduline Tit   *Anthoscopus minutus*
See page 49. Common in arid scrub in the Karoo and Kalahari.

Layard's Titbabbler   *Parisoma layardi*
See page 76. Uncommon resident in coastal, semi-arid and montane scrub.

Long-billed Crombec   *Sylvietta rufescens*
See page 52.

DESERT

Karoo Chat   *Cercomela schlegelii*
See page 80. The Namib Desert race of this chat is pale buff in colour, with darker wings and a white rump.

Tractrac Chat   *Cercomela tractrac*
See page 80. The Namib Desert race of this chat is almost entirely white with darker wings and tail.

Warblers, robins, etc.

FOREST
(This habitat includes forest edges.)

Canopy of forest

Forest tree showing canopy and mid-level

Chirinda Apalis
Apalis chirindensis

illustrated page 21
(Newman's Birds p. 341)

HABITAT: Highland evergreen forest in the eastern districts of Zimbabwe and on Mount Gorongoza in Mozambique.
STATUS: Uncommon localised resident, endemic to the above-mentioned forests.
BEHAVIOUR: Occurs in pairs or small groups. Difficult to see high up in the canopy, but its call is most distinctive. Calls throughout the day, even when other birds are quiet. Moves restlessly like other warblers as it gleans insects off the vegetation, often coming down to the middle levels and sunny patches to feed. Common in bird parties.
CALL: "Quick, quick, quick" uttered in phrases of 20-30 notes over 4-6 seconds.
DESCRIPTION: Entirely blue-grey in colour, a bit paler below with light-coloured tips to the underside of the tail feathers.

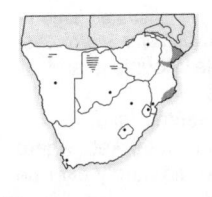

Black-headed Apalis
Apalis melanocephala

illustrated page 21
(Newman's Birds p. 341)

HABITAT: Found only in lowland evergreen forest and forest edges in parts of Mozambique and areas such as Haroni-Rusitu in Zimbabwe. Possible in the Honde Valley below Nyanga as well.
STATUS: Common resident in Mozambique, uncommon in Zimbabwe.

BEHAVIOUR: Gleans insects off leaves and branches in the canopy and mid-sections of the forest.
CALL: A fast, trilling "pee-pee-pee-pee".
DESCRIPTION: **A two-tone bird**: dark above, pale below.

Slender Bulbul
Phyllastrephus debilis

illustrated page 17
(*Newman's Birds* p. 307)

HABITAT: Very limited distribution in the lowland evergreen forests of Mozambique and along the Zimbabwe-Mozambique border.
STATUS: Common resident within its restricted range.
BEHAVIOUR: Occurs both in the canopy and the lower sections of the forest, foraging much like a warbler. Not easy to see; its presence is usually given away by its characteristic call.
CALL: A harsh "chuck, churr, churr-churr-chrrrt ...", going up the scale, getting faster and then sharply terminated.
DESCRIPTION: The problem is to recognise this as a small bulbul rather than a biggish warbler. It looks like a small version of a Yellow-streaked Bulbul, but is much paler both on the head and underparts, and its grey head is distinctive.

Forest Weaver
Ploceus bicolor

illustrated page 30
(*Newman's Birds* p. 409)

HABITAT: Coastal and inland forests.
STATUS: Common, localised resident.
BEHAVIOUR: A non-gregarious, insectivorous weaver usually found in pairs feeding in the mid-stratum of forests. A quiet species that creeps around branches and probes for its food beneath bark and into *Usnea* lichen ("old man's beard").
CALL: The song is a duet by both sexes, the most common phrase a high-pitched series of pleasant notes "fweeee, foo-fwee foo-fwee..." repeated with variations plus some soft rattling sounds.
DESCRIPTION: Adults identical, **maintaining the same plumage all year**. Race (a) is typical of southern birds, race (b) occurs in coastal southern Mozambique, northern Mozambique and nort-eastern Zimbabwe (see colour illustration on page 30). Immature is similar, the flanks with an olive wash.

──────── *Understorey of forest* ────────

Knysna Warbler
Bradypterus sylvaticus

illustrated page 19
(*Newman's Birds* p. 335)

HABITAT: Densely forested areas on Table Mountain and all along the coast to southern KwaZulu-Natal.
STATUS: Uncommon resident, endemic to South Africa.
BEHAVIOUR: Extremely secretive, hiding away in thickets where it is usually overlooked. But for its call it would hardly ever be recorded.
CALL: A high-pitched, staccato song uttered with increasing

speed and ending with a trill "tsip-tsip-tsip-tsip-tsiptsiptsiptsip-trrrrrrrrrrrrrrr".
DESCRIPTION: Very similar in appearance to Barratt's Warbler, and where both species occur, such as in the Eastern Cape coastal forests, the song is the only way to separate them.

Barratt's Warbler
Bradypterus barratti

illustrated page 19
(Newman's Birds p. 335)

HABITAT: Forest thickets and tangled vegetation along streams and kloofs, and in Zimbabwe montane forest fringes and scrub. Occurs at higher altitudes in summer, moving lower down in winter when it is found on the edges of forest, in gullies and thickets.
STATUS: Fairly common resident.
BEHAVIOUR: A secretive bird which feeds low down or on the ground, where it runs through the dense vegetation.
CALL: A series of loud notes, slow at first but getting faster "chit, chit, chatterchatter chatter chatchat" heard all day long during summer. Gives a monosyllabic "krrt" as alarm, all year. The call has the same pattern as that of the African Sedge Warbler, but is more strident.
DESCRIPTION: Dark brown with a rounded tail. Similar to the African Sedge Warbler but **does not occur in reed-beds**.

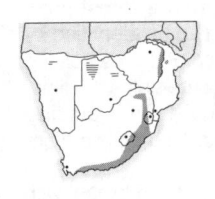

Yellow-throated Warbler
Phylloscopus ruficapillus

illustrated page 22
(Newman's Birds p. 345)

HABITAT: The middle levels, undergrowth and ground cover within forests.
STATUS: Common resident even in relatively small patches of forest.
BEHAVIOUR: Occurs singly or in pairs; often joins mixed bird parties in the forest. Feeds very actively through the trees.
CALL: A thin, high-pitched "tirritee tirritee tirritee" or "sip sip sip sip pilly pilly pilly".
DESCRIPTION: A tiny bird with a distinctive **brown cap and yellow eyebrow, throat and breast**.

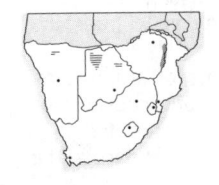

Brier Warbler
Oreophilais robertsi
Also called Roberts's Prinia

illustrated page 21
(Newman's Birds p. 359)

HABITAT: Restricted to the eastern districts of Zimbabwe and neighbouring Mozambique. A forest edge bird that also goes into the forest canopy along the edges and in strips along streams, and is **common in bramble-choked gullies**.
STATUS: Common resident.
BEHAVIOUR/CALL: Goes about in groups of 4-6 and **chatters and scolds** rather like a miniature Arrow-marked Babbler, with one bird taking over from the other or all joining in together.
DESCRIPTION: A featureless brownish grey bird with a **pale yellow eye**.

Eastern Honeyguide
Indicator meliphilus

illustrated page 17
(*Newman's Birds* p. 273)

HABITAT: Restricted to low-lying forests in the Honde Valley and Haroni-Rusitu regions of eastern Zimbabwe, plus Mozambique.
STATUS: Uncommon resident, difficult to find.
BEHAVIOUR: Generally solitary. It hawks insects from perches in the understorey and middle levels, and also gleans insects from flowers, bark and leaves. When on the lookout for food from a perch it shows a **distinctive side to side head and body movement**.
CALL: A sibilant whistle.
DESCRIPTION: Very similar in appearance to the Lesser Honeyguide, but smaller and does not have a moustachial streak. The upperparts, when seen clearly, are greener than those of the Lesser Honeyguide. The bill is much heavier than that of any warbler.

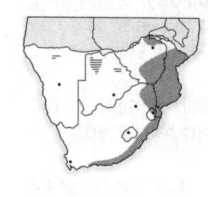

Scaly-throated Honeyguide
Indicator variegatus

illustrated page 17
(*Newman's Birds* p. 273)

HABITAT: Fringes of indigenous forest, riparian forest and densely wooded valleys.
STATUS: Uncommon resident.
BEHAVIOUR: Often hawks from a perch or from a forest path, sometimes from mixed bird parties, when it can be identified by its **white outer tail feathers**. It spends much of the day sitting quietly on a branch, being very difficult to locate unless calling.
CALL: The diagnostic call is a ventriloquial and **purring** "trrrrrrrrrrrrr", rising in pitch towards the end. Also calls a high-pitched "foyt-foyt-foyt".
DESCRIPTION: Has a stubby black bill, grey head and breast with much white and yellow speckling, pale yellow underparts and greenish wings with yellow feather edges. Sexes are alike.

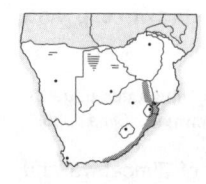

Brown Robin
Erythropygia signata

illustrated page 18
(*Newman's Birds* p. 329)

HABITAT: Indigenous forests of the eastern escarpment south of the Limpopo River as well as the eastern coastal forests.
STATUS: Uncommon endemic resident.
BEHAVIOUR: Occurs singly within the dim interior of the forest where it forages on the ground in leaf-mould, but is easily overlooked. At dusk it sings from a perch on the forest fringe, at which time it is not shy. It often sings until nearly dark and is the last diurnal bird to be heard within the forest.
CALL: The song is a melancholy series of high-pitched phrases, always beginning on a double note "tree-trooo, te-tree-too ...".
DESCRIPTION: Brown above, white below with **white eyebrows and wing markings** which are conspicuous but often difficult to see within the forest. In flight shows a white tailtip.

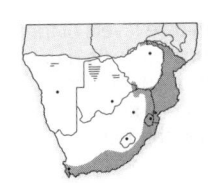

Sombre Bulbul
Andropadus importunus

illustrated page 17
(Newman's Birds p. 305)

HABITAT: Dense coastal and riparian bush, evergreen forest, forest fringes and well-wooded coastal parks and gardens.
STATUS: Common resident.
BEHAVIOUR: Single birds call from the mid-canopy of well-leaved trees within vocal contact of each other. Not a secretive species, but its cryptic colouring blends well with its leafy surroundings. In the early mornings and after rain it sometimes perches openly while calling.
CALL: The common call note "willie!" is heard throughout the year and is the best aid to its identity. The full call is heard mostly in the warmer months and has several local variations. It is a babbling trill likened to "Willie! Come out and fight! Sca-a-ared", the final phrase barely audible. In southern coastal bush the call is often shortened to "peeet" or "peeeit" which is usually answered by other birds of the same species. When agitated this call becomes "peeet peeet peeet ..." in rapid succession.
DESCRIPTION: The **creamy-white eyes** are diagnostic. The usual plumage colour throughout southern Africa is dull olive-green, upperparts slightly darker than the underparts. From the lower Zambezi northwards the colouring becomes a less sombre, brighter green.

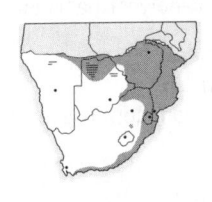

Terrestrial Bulbul
Phyllastrephus terrestris

illustrated page 17
(Newman's Birds p. 305)

HABITAT: Dense undergrowth in evergreen forests, and dense riparian, coastal bush and hillside thickets.
STATUS: Common resident.
BEHAVIOUR/CALL: It forages in small parties on the ground amid leaf-litter, and also in the lower vegetation levels, while maintaining a **continual, quiet chattering**: rather gruff, short disjointed notes, but longer strophes when agitated. Individuals also forage briefly on the lower sections of tree trunks.
DESCRIPTION: Few diagnostic markings. The entire upperparts from below the eyes are a uniform olive-brown, this extending onto the flanks; in contrast the throat is white but the rest of the underparts are dull buffy-white or greyish. The pale yellow gape can be seen only at close range. In northern Botswana and Zimbabwe this species is larger and paler, the upperparts more reddish brown.

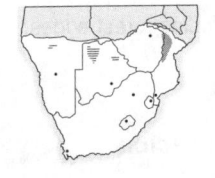

Stripe-cheeked Bulbul
Andropadus milanjensis

illustrated page 17
(Newman's Birds p. 307)

HABITAT: Restricted to the north-eastern Zimbabwe-Mozambique border region, where it inhabits evergreen forests and dense forest scrub and thickets.
STATUS: Common resident in eastern highland forests.
BEHAVIOUR: It forages in the forest canopy where it is usually

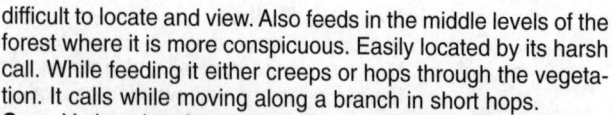

difficult to locate and view. Also feeds in the middle levels of the forest where it is more conspicuous. Easily located by its harsh call. While feeding it either creeps or hops through the vegetation. It calls while moving along a branch in short hops.
CALL: Various harsh calls "chuck, churr, chuck-churr-churr".
DESCRIPTION: The underparts are a much greener yellow than in the Yellow-bellied Bulbul. Distinguished from all other bulbuls by its **grey head, dark eyes with white eyelids** and, at close range, faint white streaks on the cheeks and ear coverts.

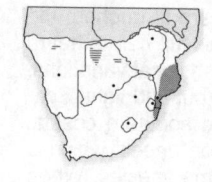

Rudd's Apalis
Apalis ruddi

illustrated page 20
(*Newman's Birds* p. 341)

HABITAT: Restricted to dense woodland, coastal bush and dune forest in the east, preferring dense thickets overgrown with creepers.
STATUS: Uncommon resident.
BEHAVIOUR: Occurs singly or in pairs, and feeds actively in thickets.
CALL: A fast, loud "tritritritritritrit ..." by one bird, the other calling at the same time (but out of phase) "punk-punk- punk ...".
DESCRIPTION: Differs from the Bar-throated Apalis in the dark eye, yellowish under-tail and lack of white in outer tail feathers.

Bar-throated Apalis   *Apalis thoracica*
See page 54. This tiny bird occurs in a variety of habitats including forest edges.

Bleating Warbler   *Camaroptera brachyura*
See page 55. The Green-backed form is common in evergreen and riverine forest.

Cape Penduline Tit   *Anthoscopus minutus*
See page 49. Various habitats including coastal bush.

Neddicky   *Cisticola fulvicapilla*
See page 44. Common in a wide range of habitats including coastal bush.

Slender Bulbul   *Phyllastrephus debilis*
See page 84. A small bulbul with a very limited distribution in the evergreen forests along the Zimbabwe-Mozambique border.

Tawny-flanked Prinia   *Prinia subflava*
See page 60. Occurs in most habitats including forest edges.

SUBURBIA

Bar-throated Apalis   *Apalis thoracica*
See page 54.

Black-chested Prinia *Prinia flavicans*
See page 62.

Dusky Flycatcher *Muscicapa adusta*
See page 50. Occurs in well-wooded parks and gardens.

European Marsh Warbler *Acrocephalus palustris*
See page 56. Comes into garden hedges but keeps well hidden.

Garden Warbler *Sylvia borin*
See page 55. Enters gardens, where it loves mulberries.

Greater Honeyguide *Indicator indicator*
See page 46. Occurs in well-wooded suburbia.

Lesser Honeyguide *Indicator minor*
See page 46. Visits gardens.

Mountain Chat *Oenanthe monticola*
See page 62. Visits gardens in some parts of its range. The female may cause confusion.

Namaqua Warbler *Phragmacia substriata*
Previously called Namaqua Prinia.
See page 81. Frequents gardens in parts of its range.

Sharp-billed Honeyguide *Prodotiscus regulus*
See page 45.

Sombre Bulbul *Andropadus importunus*
See page 87. Well-wooded coastal parks and gardens.

Spotted Flycatcher *Muscicapa striata*
See page 50. Occurs in well-wooded parks and gardens.

Tawny-flanked Prinia *Prinia subflava*
See page 60. Common in gardens, especially in winter.

Terrestrial Bulbul *Phyllastrephus terrestris*
See page 87. Found in dense thickets in coastal bush.

White-browed Scrub Robin *Erythropygia leucophrys*
See page 56. A common resident in coastal bush.

Willow Warbler *Phylloscopus trochilus*
See page 43.

Yellow-breasted Apalis *Apalis flavida*
See page 59. Edge of evergreen and riverine forest.

• LARKS •

WOODLAND
(This habitat includes grassland with scattered bushes and stony open woodland.)

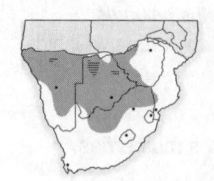

Monotonous Lark
Mirafra passerina

illustrated page 25
(*Newman's Birds* p. 277)

HABITAT: Stony areas, open woodland such as mopane, and acacia scrub in the drier parts of the subregion.
STATUS: Nomadic, moving into areas in response to rain. Common resident at these times.
BEHAVIOUR: A small bird, easily overlooked when not calling. A displaying male calls from a perch on some low bush or termite mound, or in flight, and it does all this with its plumage fluffed. When flushed this lark takes off in jinking flight but quickly drops back into the grass.
CALL: Only heard in midsummer after rain. A monotonous four-syllable phrase likened to the words "sugar is sweet" or "three to meet you"; the first and third notes are lower than the second and fourth. Often many males can be heard calling at the same time.
DESCRIPTION: In flight shows rufous in the outer wings. Its white throat is conspicuous when the bird is calling, contrasting with its buffy breast. Does not occur in the same areas as the Melodious Lark.

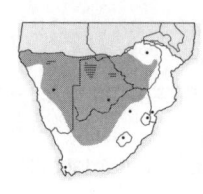

Fawn-coloured Lark
Mirafra africanoides

illustrated page 25
(*Newman's Birds* p. 277)

HABITAT: Broad-leaved woodland edges and thornveld, mainly on Kalahari sands.
STATUS: Common resident.
BEHAVIOUR/CALL: Conspicuous and confiding, and **always found on sandy soils**. Forages in the open but flies into a tree when disturbed. Sings in a hunched posture from a tree-top or in cruising flight, a jumbled series of **harsh staccato chips and twitterings ending in a buzzy slur**.
DESCRIPTION: A medium-sized lark. Its underparts are white, streaked brown on the upper breast; upperparts fawn-coloured to rich rufous according to locality, and **streaked darker** overall (not mottled as in the Sabota Lark). In the west can be confused with the Karoo Lark, which however has a dark line through the eye.

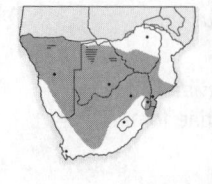

Sabota Lark
Mirafra sabota

illustrated page 25
(*Newman's Birds* p. 279)

HABITAT: Mainly drier woodland with sparse ground cover or stony ground.
STATUS: Common resident.

BEHAVIOUR: In common with a few others of its genus it has a distinctly **crouched jizz**, always with its legs flexed and its body held close to the horizontal. It forages on the ground on dirt tracks and roads, seldom far from bushes, or perches on top of a bush or small tree while singing. It may also sing in hovering flight.
CALL: The song is **melodious and variable** and incorporates the song phrases of many other birds.
DESCRIPTION: In all its regional variations this medium-sized lark has **boldly mottled upperparts** and a **prominent white eyebrow** extending from the base of its bill to well behind its eye. It also has **white below the eye**, and buffy outer tail feathers. Its **underparts are entirely white** except for bold breast-spots.

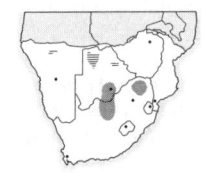

Short-clawed Lark   illustrated page 26
Certhilauda chuana   (*Newman's Birds* p. 281)
HABITAT: Dry thornveld in a restricted range that extends from just south of Louis Trichardt south-westwards almost to the Orange River, and into eastern Botswana.
STATUS: Uncommon resident.
BEHAVIOUR: If not on the ground, it will be calling from the top of a bush. It has a shriller call than the Rufous-naped Lark, and does not flick its wings after calling.
CALL: A shrill "pheeee, pheeoo-pheeoo, phew, pheeoo-pheeit ...". In its display flight it calls a drawn-out "pooooeeeee".
DESCRIPTION: Not an easy lark to identify, certainly not on plumage. The illustration in *Newman's Birds* shows its typical jizz, always with the bill pointing slightly upwards, rather like a pipit. It has a more **slender bill** than the Rufous-naped Lark, and shows no rusty crown feathers. If you are outside the range described above, you are not looking at a Short-clawed Lark.

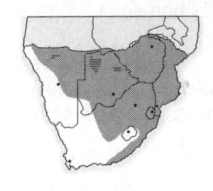

Rufous-naped Lark   illustrated page 25
Mirafra africana   (*Newman's Birds* p. 279)
HABITAT: Grassland with scattered bushes and termite mounds for perches.
STATUS: Common resident.
BEHAVIOUR: Usually heard before it is seen. Its call is one of the most familiar sounds along our country roads, as it often calls from a fence post. It also calls from the tops of small bushes and even termite mounds, and it does so daily in fair weather for about nine months of the year. After every second or third call it raises its **rusty crest and shakes its wings, producing a few soft claps**. Because of this behaviour and its distinctive call it is one of the easiest larks to identify.
CALL: A rather melancholy "tseep-see ooo" which is fairly far-carrying. Also utters a song containing imitations of other bird-songs while making aerial cruises at dusk.

DESCRIPTION: A medium-sized to large lark with a rufous nape and rufous edges to the wing feathers, but these are only obvious at close range. Has a small crest.

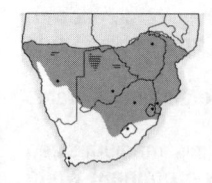

Chestnut-backed Finchlark
Eremopterix leucotis

illustrated page 26
(*Newman's Birds* p. 287)

HABITAT: Open areas in bushveld; also airstrips, burnt grassland and gravel flats.
STATUS: Common resident, nomadic in many areas.
BEHAVIOUR: Always in small flocks which wheel around in jinking flight, then suddenly settle. On the ground it runs with erect posture; feeds with the body held horizontally.
CALL: A sharp, rattling call "chip cheew" and sparrow-like chirps in fluttering flight.
DESCRIPTION: The **well-mottled female** is usually accompanied by the distinctive males with their chestnut upperparts, black body and **white ear-patch and thighs**.

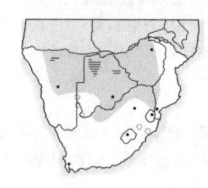

Dusky Lark
Pinarocorys nigricans

illustrated page 26
(*Newman's Birds* p. 281)

HABITAT: Mixed bushveld or open woodland with a grassy understorey.
STATUS: Uncommon non-breeding summer visitor.
BEHAVIOUR: Usually seen in scattered flocks. Jizz fairly erect: **thrush-like**. It forages on the ground, walking quickly, then stopping and flicking its wings before walking on. Its flight is markedly undulating. Also has a display flight in which it spirals upwards and then circles, flapping and gliding, before descending in a series of stalling dives to settle in a tree.
CALL: Throughout the display it calls "zhree". Otherwise a rather silent bird.
DESCRIPTION: A fairly large lark. The bold facial and breast markings **resemble those of a Groundscraper Thrush**, but its upperparts are much darker and the bill is heavier.

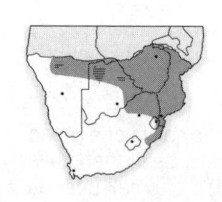

Flappet Lark
Mirafra rufocinnamomea

illustrated page 25
(*Newman's Birds* p. 281)

HABITAT: Clearings in open woodland; hilly grassland with scattered bushes and rocks, and coastal grassland.
STATUS: Common resident.
BEHAVIOUR/CALL: Easily overlooked unless performing its display flight, which may occur at any time: a **high aerial cruise in which it performs bouts of wing-clapping** that produce a muffled "prrrrrrr, prrrrrrr", audible in quiet, windless conditions such as in the early morning. Difficult to spot in the air, but at the end of its display it dives to near the ground and then levels off before settling. Utters a soft "tuee-tui", but does not call while flying. On the ground it runs away quickly from the observer and is reluctant to flush.

DESCRIPTION: Compact appearance and, on the ground, the **whitish feather-edges** of its folded wings and its short tail aid identification.

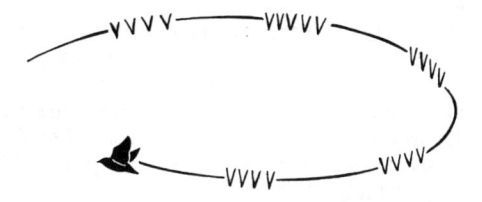

Display flight pattern of Flappet Lark

GRASSLAND AND MARSHLAND

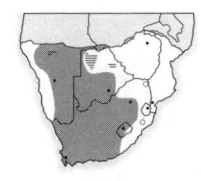

Clapper Lark
Mirafra apiata

illustrated page 25
(*Newman's Birds* p. 281)

HABITAT: Mainly grassland, but also semi-arid areas with low shrubs, and fynbos in the south-western Cape.
STATUS: Common widespread resident.
BEHAVIOUR/CALL: Most easily located and identified by its characteristic territorial display (October-February). At other times it is unobtrusive. In display the male flies upwards a few metres, hovers briefly with sharp wing-clapping, then drops steeply while uttering a long drawn-out "fooeeeeee". The call is audible up to half a kilometre away and can hardly go unnoticed.
DESCRIPTION: A medium-sized lark. On the ground it can be told from the Flappet Lark only with difficulty since there are several local forms with plumage varying between dark and pale.

Display flight pattern of Clapper Lark

Long-billed Lark
Certhilauda curvirostris

illustrated page 25
(*Newman's Birds* p. 283)

HABITAT: Overgrazed highveld grassland, stony ridges in grassland and in the Karoo; also Namib dunes.
STATUS: Common resident.
BEHAVIOUR/CALL: Forages by digging with its long bill, stooped forward with legs flexed, or stands on rocks with erect stance from where it may whistle a long "peeeeeeeoo" with descending cadence. Also calls from the ground "pheeoopeeoo", the calls always having a marked ventriloquial quality. In display the male rises steeply into the air, then plummets down while calling a loud "cheeoooo".
DESCRIPTION: A large lark. Plumage colours vary greatly from region to region but its large size, erect jizz and long bill are unmistakable.

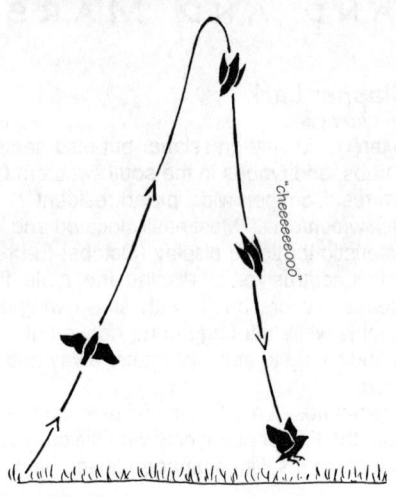

Display flight pattern of Long-billed Lark

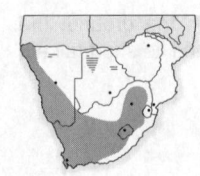

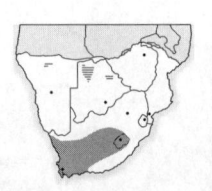

Thick-billed Lark
Galerida magnirostris

illustrated page 26
(*Newman's Birds* p. 283)

HABITAT: Montane grassland, Karoo, fynbos and Cape wheat fields.
STATUS: Common resident.
BEHAVIOUR: Occurs commonly on roadside verges where it forages on flexed legs. Sings its short song phrases either in flight or from a post, rock, termite mound or bush.
CALL: The usual song is "chit trit triddlywit" with variations, very musical.
DESCRIPTION: The **thick bill and well-streaked breast** plus large size are diagnostic.

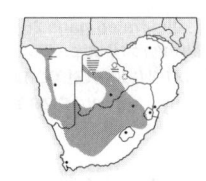

Pink-billed Lark
Spizocorys conirostris

Illustrated page 26
(*Newman's Birds* p. 285)

HABITAT: Patches of open ground in short grassland and farmlands; has a wide inland distribution.
STATUS: Common resident; nomadic.
BEHAVIOUR: Usually seen in small flocks. It runs in short bursts with erect jizz while foraging.
CALL: In flight it repeats a soft "see see see".
DESCRIPTION: A small lark. The **stout conical pink bill** is diagnostic. It differs from Botha's Lark in the **white throat and buffy underparts**, the breast with a few dark spots not extending to the flanks. The outer tail feathers are buff.

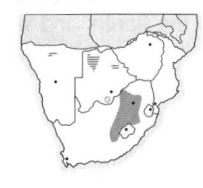

Melodious Lark
Mirafra cheniana

illustrated page 25
(*Newman's Birds* p. 277)

HABITAT: Dense grassland with scattered bushes.
STATUS: Common resident within its restricted range.
BEHAVIOUR/CALL: It has a repetitive "chuck chuck chucker" alarm call and a lively but rambling song, which mostly mimics the songs of other birds. Whether singing from a perch or in territorial display it **fluffs its plumage**. In display the bird rises to a considerable height on whirring wings, and circles for periods of 10-20 minutes, **alternately fluttering and singing while dipping and rising**; it sometimes completes the display with a sudden descent into the grass. It also spends much time **chasing others of its kind** during the summer breeding period.
DESCRIPTION: A smallish lark. When singing from a perch the white throat contrasts with the buffy breast and belly. In flight it shows rufous outer wing panels and white outer tail feathers. Outside the summer breeding season it is quite inconspicuous. Its range does not overlap with that of the similar Monotonous Lark.

Rudd's Lark
Heteromirafra ruddi

illustrated page 26
(*Newman's Birds* p. 285)

HABITAT: Short grassland only at altitudes of 1 700 m or more, preferably **well-grassed hilltops**.
STATUS: Uncommon, localised resident.
BEHAVIOUR/CALL: Elusive and largely terrestrial. It runs quickly among the grass tufts and is very difficult to locate. Does not flush easily or perch. Best located in midsummer when it displays by flying high for long periods calling "pitchoo chereee, pitchoo chreee".
DESCRIPTION: This is one of the smallest larks. In flight it shows white outer tail feathers. On the ground it stands erect with a long-legged appearance. It appears large-headed and has a short and narrow tail.

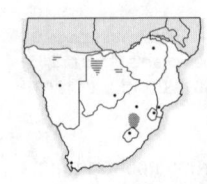

Botha's Lark   illustrated page 26
Spizocorys fringillaris   (*Newman's Birds* p. 285)

HABITAT: Highly localised in the Amersfoort-Wakkerstroom region of Mpumalanga where it occurs patchily in overgrazed uplands.
STATUS: Uncommon, localised resident.
BEHAVIOUR: Inconspicuous. A small lark that feeds in pairs or small groups, darting about with an upright stance, flushing readily.
CALL: The only calls are a cheerful "cheree" plus "chuck" while flying.
DESCRIPTION: In flight its fanned tail reveals buff outer feathers. Although its bill is pinkish red it differs from the Pink-billed Lark in having **breast-spotting that extends to the flanks** and in being darker on the upperparts.

Red-capped Lark   *Calandrella cinerea*
See below.

Rufous-naped Lark   *Mirafra africana*
See page 91.

Spike-heeled Lark   *Chersomanes albofasciata*
See opposite. Frequents grassland in the east of its range.

FYNBOS

Clapper Lark   *Mirafra apiata*
See page 93. In the Cape occurs mainly in mountain fynbos.

Thick-billed Lark   *Galerida magnirostris*
See page 94. Occurs in fynbos and croplands in the south-western Cape.

KAROO AND SEMI-ARID AREAS
(This habitat includes gravel plains, dry pan fringes and shrubby semi-desert.)

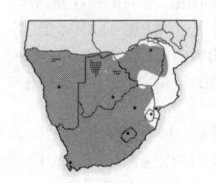

Red-capped Lark   illustrated page 26
Calandrella cinerea   (*Newman's Birds* p. 283)

HABITAT: Stony fringes of dry pans, airstrips, grassland (especially burnt or overgrazed) and semi-desert.
STATUS: Common resident; nomadic in most areas, but these movements are not well understood.
BEHAVIOUR: In summer normally in pairs or small groups, but in the dry season occurs in fossil riverbeds of the central Kalahari in flocks of many hundreds. Walks on the ground or

makes short runs; it flies off low if flushed, but is normally fairly confiding.
CALL: In early summer the male sings from the ground or in flight, a sequence of high-pitched notes in which a trilled "treee" is prominent.
DESCRIPTION: A medium-sized lark. On the ground easily told by its rufous head-crest and shoulder patches.

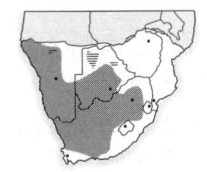

Spike-heeled Lark
Chersomanes albofasciata

illustrated page 26
(*Newman's Birds* p. 283)

HABITAT: Grassland in the east of its range, but more sparsely grassed regions and shrubby semi-desert in the west.
STATUS: Common resident.
BEHAVIOUR: Singly or in small groups. Largely terrestrial. Runs about quickly while foraging, its **erect stance, short tail and slender, slightly decurved bill** being diagnostic. When disturbed it flies a short distance only (at which time the white tailtip can be seen) and will sometimes settle on a low shrub.
CALL: It has a low display flight from which it glides down with raised wings while calling "trrrt trrrt trrrt". On the ground several birds may interact while calling collectively, a shrill, excitable "trrr trrr trrr chee chee …".
Description: A medium-sized lark with a diagnostic **white tip to the short, slender tail**.

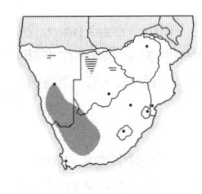

Black-eared Finchlark
Eremopterix australis

illustrated page 26
(*Newman's Birds* p. 287)

HABITAT: Gravel plains, Karoo scrub and red Kalahari sandveld.
STATUS: Uncommon resident; highly nomadic.
BEHAVIOUR: Highly gregarious; always in flocks, often large, which forage among shrubs and rocks in arid areas. They flush readily, making off with the erratic flight typical of finchlarks.
CALL: In flight individuals call "chip chip" or "preep preep".
DESCRIPTION: A small species. On the ground easily identified by the blackish males. In the air **males appear completely black** while females show **white bellies**, not black like other female finchlarks.

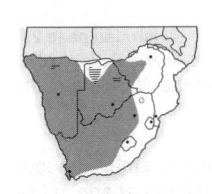

Grey-backed Finchlark
Eremopterix verticalis

illustrated page 26
(*Newman's Birds* p. 287)

HABITAT: The drier regions; often in burnt areas, **around dry pans** and in farmlands.
STATUS: Common resident; nomadic.
BEHAVIOUR: **Normally in scattered flocks** that forage in the open. If disturbed, flocks take off and circle in typically erratic, jerky flight but soon resettle.
CALL: A sharp chirp.
DESCRIPTION: Like other finchlarks this species is best identified

by the predominantly black males which have **white patches on their crowns and ear coverts** (the male Chestnut-backed Finchlark has no white on its crown).

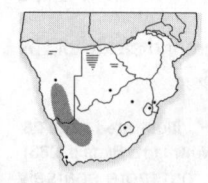

Sclater's Lark
Spizocorys sclateri

illustrated page 26
(*Newman's Birds* p. 285)

HABITAT: Arid stony plains and shrubland from the Karoo to southern Namibia.
STATUS: Uncommon localised resident.
BEHAVIOUR: Difficult to find, but usually occurs in small groups that are most easily seen when they fly to water. Drinks often.
CALL: In flight a repeated "trrrt trrrt ...".
DESCRIPTION: This small lark's diagnostic feature is the **black mark below the eye** which can only be seen at close range.

Stark's Lark *Eremalauda starki*
See below. A nomadic species found in the Karoo and the Namib.

Thick-billed Lark *Galerida magnirostris*
See page 94. A common resident in the Karoo.

DESERT

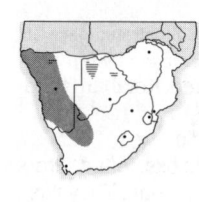

Stark's Lark
Eremalauda starki

illustrated page 26
(*Newman's Birds* p. 285)

HABITAT: Shrubby semi-desert and sparsely grassed gravel plains in the Namib Desert.
STATUS: Common resident; nomadic.
BEHAVIOUR/CALL: Nearly always in flocks, sometimes huge. Individuals forage on flexed legs while pecking in the sand for seeds. May sing from the ground, a **trilled melody of mixed notes**, or in display flight while circling high, before plunging directly to the ground. The normal flight call is an occasional "chrree".
DESCRIPTION: A smallish lark. Diagnostic feature is the erectile crest that imparts a **peaked appearance to the head**.

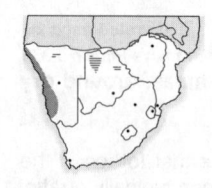

Gray's Lark
Ammomanes grayi

illustrated page 26
(*Newman's Birds* p. 285)

HABITAT: Confined to the arid gravel flats of the Namib Desert extending almost to the coast.
STATUS: Common localised resident.
BEHAVIOUR: Forages on the ground in pairs or small groups. Unless moving is extremely difficult to see. Seeks shade in the heat of the day beside stones or in rodent burrows.
CALL: It sings mostly before dawn, a high-pitched "si si chew chew chew chew, chweetit, chweetit ...". The normal flight call is "tseet".

DESCRIPTION: Palest of the larks, appearing almost white in the field.

The four red-backed larks

The Red Lark, Dune Lark, Barlow's Lark and Karoo Lark are all so similar that for the uninitiated confusion is almost inevitable. In fact confusion reigned in ornithological circles for many years. It was only in the 1990s that comprehensive studies, based on genetic, behavioural and morphological criteria, established that a previously unknown and unnamed species exists: Barlow's Lark. We are indebted to researchers at the FitzPatrick Institute of African Ornithology for unravelling the mystery, and for an article by Dr Peter Ryan, one of the researchers, published in Africa: Birds and Birding *Volume 1, No 4, for the information about the red-backed larks on these pages. Readers are urged to consult that work in order to study the illustrations of these birds.*

All four larks in the complex have dune-red to reddish brown upperparts: all have white eyebrows extending from the base of the bill to behind the eye and all have a black line through the lores. In all the underparts are basically white with a variable amount of dark streaking on the breast. **Specific identification rests in the degree of dark streaking (dark feather centres) on the bird's upper- and underparts.** *There is also some small variation in size between species, and even in tail and bill length, but these differences are slight and probably of little help without direct comparison. Males are also larger than females.*

These larks occupy discrete ranges (see distribution maps). The only zone of overlap is near Port Nolloth, where Barlow's Lark and the Karoo Lark meet. All four species inhabit arid and semi-arid scrubland, and all but the Dune Lark also occur in rocky areas provided there is some loose soil. They use their bills to dig for food in the sand, often around the base of vegetation. They rest in shade during the heat of the day. If disturbed they walk away from the observer, using vegetation for cover. They may perch on low bushes for a better view of the observer and to utter their rattling alarm call. In flight display the males climb high, singing continuously while circling slowly or beating into the wind. The normal song phrase is similar in all four species, consisting of a few "chip chip chip ..." lead-in notes (2-5 or more according to species) followed by a whistle and a terminal trill. The entire sequence is delivered rapidly, lasts 1-2 seconds and is repeated monotonously every 2-5 seconds.

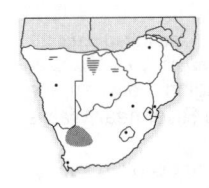

Red Lark
Certhilauda burra

illustrated page 25
(*Newman's Birds* p. 279)

HABITAT: Well-vegetated red sand dunes and scrub-lined, sandy washes and plains south of the Orange River in Bushmanland.

DESCRIPTION: This is the largest form. There are three races: *C.b. burra* from the red dunes in the north and east of its range has a **uniform brick-red back without any dark streaking** above. Birds from the central and southern parts of its range (*C.b. harei*) are **browner and variably streaked above**. All are very heavily blotched on the breast, but the **flanks and belly are plain** except for birds from the eastern dunes around Van Wyksvlei (*C.b. aridula*) which have **some streaking on the flanks**. It has a **short, deep bill which appears stubby**, a longer tail than the other three species of red-backed larks and a heavy flight action. In the Brandvlei region, where the brown, streaky-backed race can be confused with nearby populations of the Karoo Lark, the heavier bill and plain white belly of the Red Lark are the best identification features. However, the distributions of the two species do not overlap.

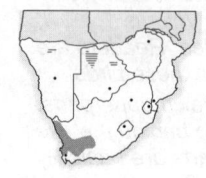

Karoo Lark
Certhilauda albescens

illustrated page 25
(*Newman's Birds* p. 279)

HABITAT AND DESCRIPTION: This, the smallest and most widespread of the four red-backed larks, has a **slender, slightly decurved bill**. It is told from the other species by **breast streaking extending onto the belly, primarily along the flanks**, and onto the under-tail coverts. There is also **heavy streaking on the upperparts**. The basic colour of the upperparts changes with soil colour. Birds of the pale coastal sands (*C.a. albescens* and *codea*) are **pale grey-brown**, becoming **rich rufous-brown and red** in the western interior (*C.a. guttata*), and grading into **dark chocolate-brown** in the eastern Karoo (*C.a. karruensis*). Areas of possible confusion occur north of Vanrhynsdorp where the reddest Karoo Larks tend to resemble Red Larks (check for streaking on the flanks), and at the point of overlap near Port Nolloth where this species meets Barlow's Lark.

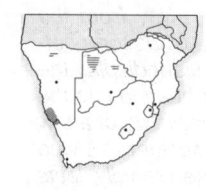

Barlow's Lark
Certhilauda barlowi

illustrated page 25
(*Newman's Birds* p. 279)

HABITAT AND DESCRIPTION: This lark tends to have the longest bill of the four, although this is variable. The plumage is also variable from **red above in the interior** (*C.b. cavei*) to **grey, brown or pink above along the coast** (*C.b. patei*). **Further north they are sandy-red above** (*C.b. barlowi*) and can closely resemble Dune Larks. The crucial identification feature is the lack of streaking on the flanks and belly, but this can be difficult to see when the feathers are old and worn.

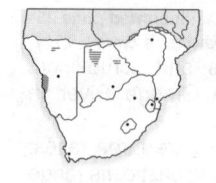

Dune Lark
Certhilauda erythroclamys

illustrated page 25
(*Newman's Birds* p. 279)

HABITAT: Dunes in the broad coastal region between the Koichab River near Lüderitz and the Kuiseb River near Walvis Bay.

DESCRIPTION: Like the dunes it inhabits, this lark is plain sandy-red above. It is also the least streaked form, having **only a few small breast streaks and virtually no streaking above**. Also, in comparison to the other three species, the malar and moustachial streaks are pale and not well defined; a useful comparison with the well-defined facial markings of Barlow's Lark to the south of the Koichab River. Another useful feature is the Dune Lark's relatively long tarsus, which gives it a lanky appearance.

Long-billed Lark *Certhilauda curvirostris*
See page 94. Found in Namib dunes.

• PIPITS •

Pipit field characters

STREAKED BACK: *Grassveld, Long-billed, Wood, Mountain, Striped, Yellow-breasted, Tree (all medium to large pipits); Short-tailed, Bushveld (small pipits).*

PLAIN BACK: *Rock, Plain-backed, Buffy.*

HEAVY STREAKING ON BREAST: *Grassveld, Mountain, Short-tailed, Tree, Bushveld, Striped.*

LIGHT STREAKING ON BREAST: *Long-billed, Wood, Plain-backed, Yellow-breasted (non-breeding).*

VERY FAINT OR NO STREAKING ON BREAST: *Rock, Buffy.*

WHITE OUTER TAIL FEATHERS: *Grassveld, Tree, Bushveld, Striped, Short-tailed.*

BUFF OUTER TAIL FEATHERS: *Rock, Long-tailed, Wood, Plain-backed, Buffy, Mountain, Yellow-breasted.*

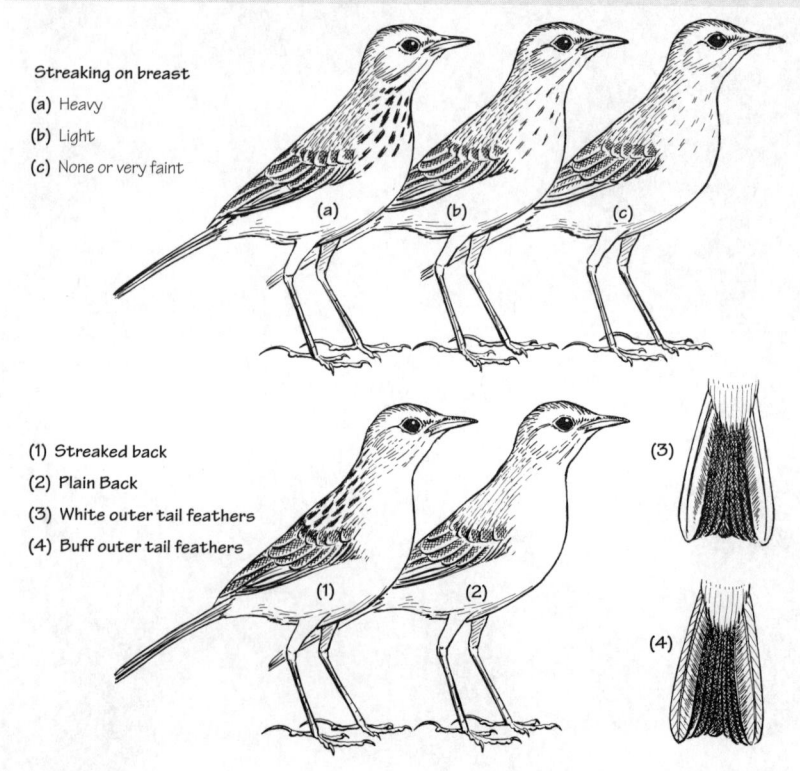

Streaking on breast
(a) Heavy
(b) Light
(c) None or very faint

(1) Streaked back
(2) Plain Back
(3) White outer tail feathers
(4) Buff outer tail feathers

Field characters of pipits

WOODLAND

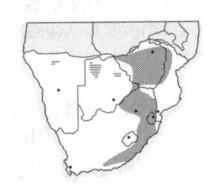

Striped Pipit
Anthus lineiventris　　　　　　　　illustrated page 27
　　　　　　　　　　　　　　　　(*Newman's Birds* p. 291)
HABITAT: Mainly rocky areas in broad-leaved woodland, rocky slopes and road cuttings within woodland, and along rocky banks of small rivers.
STATUS: Common resident.
BEHAVIOUR: Feeds on the ground among the rocks, and when disturbed flies up into the lower branches of the trees. **It has the peculiar habit of perching lengthways along a branch**, and walks confidently among the branches.
CALL: Mainly silent, but at the start of the breeding season it sings from a tree: a loud, whistling, thrush-like song.
DESCRIPTION: Distinctive with a **heavily streaked breast, the streaking extending right down to the belly and flanks, and yellow-green edging on the wing and tail feathers**. The outer tail feathers are white.

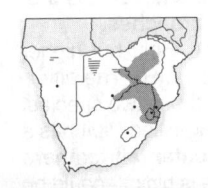

Bushveld Pipit
Anthus caffer　　　　　　　　　　illustrated page 27
　　　　　　　　　　　　　　　　(*Newman's Birds* p. 291)
HABITAT: Dry woodland and thornveld.
STATUS: Fairly common resident.
BEHAVIOUR/CALL: An inconspicuous species, often overlooked. When feeding on the ground it can easily be mistaken for a female widow (*Euplectes* species) but gives a distinctive "tshweep" call which draws attention. It is **usually found on the ground, but flies up into a tree as soon as it is disturbed**. The flight is quick but erratic. During the breeding season it sings from the trees "skeer-trurp, skeer-trurp, skeer-trurp-skee-skee".
DESCRIPTION: A small, stocky pipit, easily mistaken for a Tree Pipit, but is smaller and the underparts including the throat are more buffy coloured; the breast markings are not as well defined. The head and back are heavily streaked and the outer tail feathers are white.

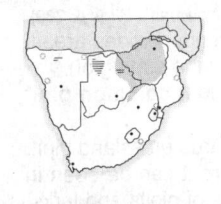

Tree Pipit
Anthus trivialis　　　　　　　　　illustrated page 27
　　　　　　　　　　　　　　　　(*Newman's Birds* p. 291)
HABITAT: Broad-leaved woodland, forest edges, grassy hillsides with occasional bushes and the edges of exotic plantations.
STATUS: Uncommon non-breeding summer visitor, occurring from late October or early November to mid- or late March. Common in the eastern highlands of Zimbabwe.
BEHAVIOUR: Generally seen singly or in pairs, but small groups may form during migration. It has a **distinctive manner of walking with its legs bent almost double and the belly close to the ground**, looking as if it is walking on its tarsus

rather than on its toes, and taking very deliberate steps. In between walking or making short runs, it pauses and bobs its tail. When disturbed it flies up into the trees where it walks among the branches.

CALL: A nasal "teez" **as it flies up**.

DESCRIPTION: It is finely streaked on the head and back and has a **distinctive white throat**. The breast is heavily streaked with tear-shaped spots. The outer tail feathers are white, as is the eyebrow.

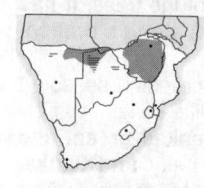

Wood Pipit
Anthus nyassae

illustrated page 27
(*Newman's Birds* p. 289)

HABITAT: Restricted to broad-leaved (miombo) woodland in Zimbabwe and broad-leaved woodland in parts of Namibia and northern Botswana.

STATUS: Fairly common to common resident. Previously regarded as a race of the Long-billed Pipit.

BEHAVIOUR: It feeds on the ground in open grassy areas beneath the trees. **Flies up into the trees whenever it is disturbed, and walks confidently along the branches**.

CALL: Very similar to that of the Long-billed Pipit, but higher pitched, slightly slower and some notes are varied. The different habitat and distribution help to separate these two species.

DESCRIPTION: Has a **white eyebrow** (the Long-billed Pipit has a buff eyebrow) and the back is darker. The **outer tail feathers are buff** and the base of the lower mandible is pink. It could be confused with the Striped Pipit which is also common in broad-leaved woodland, but the latter prefers rocky areas and has white outer tail feathers.

GRASSLAND AND MARSHLAND

Open grassland

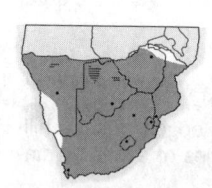

Grassveld Pipit
Anthus cinnamomeus

illustrated page 27
(*Newman's Birds* p. 289)

HABITAT: Open short grassland, cultivated lands, eroded areas, airstrips and even playing fields throughout the subregion.

STATUS: Common resident; probably the **most common pipit** in southern Africa.

BEHAVIOUR: As its name suggests this is a true grassland pipit. It is attracted to recently burnt areas where it can be seen in large numbers, together with other species of pipits and larks. It runs actively along the ground, but only for short distances, standing upright each time it stops, and often moving the tail up and down a few times.

CALL: It has a **distinctive song and a buoyant display flight**. The song "chree-chree-chree-chree-chree-chree" is repeated rapidly over and over during the dipping flight: after an upward swoop the bird drops to the ground, still calling "chree-chree-chree" continuously. The call is a single "chissik" given as the bird flies up when disturbed.

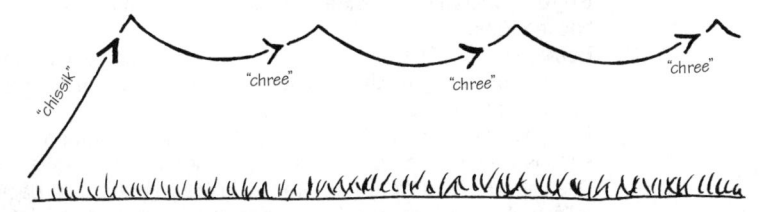

Display flight pattern of Grassveld Pipit

DESCRIPTION: The distinctive **white outer tail feathers and clear streaking on the breast**, combined with habitat and behaviour, make this a relatively easy pipit to identify. The yellow base of the lower mandible is visible at close range. Problems can occur in the alpine grassland in the Drakensberg where the very similar Mountain Pipit occurs.

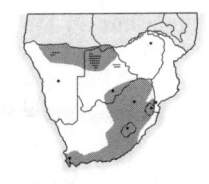

Plain-backed Pipit
Anthus leucophrys

illustrated page 27
(*Newman's Birds* p. 289)

HABITAT: The northern population occurs on floodplains in the Okavango and Caprivi, and just extends into Zimbabwe on the Zambezi floodplain at Kazungula. The southern population is found in short grassland areas, particularly in hilly regions, and favours overgrazed or burnt grassland. It is also common in cultivated lands, and visits gardens along the coast in areas such as Transkei.

STATUS: Fairly common resident.

BEHAVIOUR/CALL: Its display flight is very similar to that of the Grassveld Pipit, but it **does not sing during this circular flight**, and then drops abruptly to the ground while giving a tripping "ttt-tit" call. The song, **given from the ground or a low perch**, is "jhreet-jhree", the second note higher pitched, or often a single "jhreet", or "jhreet-jhroot". In flight it may give a single "chissik" note.

DESCRIPTION: The **plain, unstreaked back, indistinct breast markings and buffy outer tail feathers** distinguish this species from the Grassveld Pipit. It also lacks the conspicuous malar streak of the Grassveld Pipit. It is, however, easily confused with the Buffy Pipit which occurs in similar habitats. The base of the lower mandible is yellow.

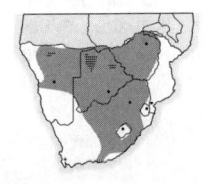

Buffy Pipit
Anthus vaalensis

illustrated page 27
(*Newman's Birds* p. 289)

HABITAT: Seems to favour drier country than the Plain-backed Pipit, but the two may occur together. It is found mainly in overgrazed areas or areas of short, patchy grassland, especially where there are termite mounds or rocks which it can use as observation posts. Attracted to burnt ground, airstrips and cultivated lands.

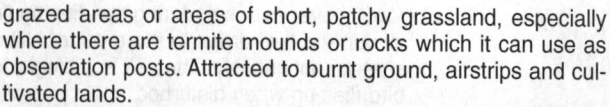

STATUS: Uncommon resident; less common than the Plain-backed Pipit.

BEHAVIOUR: It will walk or run a short distance, pause and **stand very upright with chest thrown out and bobbing its tail in a very deliberate manner**.

CALL: Gives a "chissik" call in flight or when disturbed. The song is a slow "cheroo ... chrit-chrit ... cheroo".

DESCRIPTION: Told from the Grassveld Pipit by its plain back, buffy outer tail feathers, faint breast markings and lack of a malar stripe. It is difficult to distinguish from the Plain-backed Pipit, but it has a buff or yellowish look to the upperparts (the Plain-backed Pipit has a greyish back). The base of the lower mandible is pink (yellow in the Plain-backed and Grassveld Pipits).

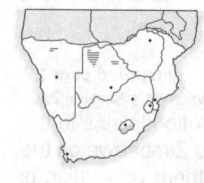

Mountain Pipit
Anthus hoeschi

illustrated page 27
(*Newman's Birds* p. 289)

HABITAT: Breeds in **high-altitude alpine grassland in the Drakensberg above 2 000 m**. A good place to find this pipit is Sani Pass. It may move down to lower altitudes to feed and can then be found together with the Grassveld Pipit, causing considerable identification problems.

STATUS: Fairly common, localised summer resident.

BEHAVIOUR/CALL: The display flight is similar to that of the Grassveld Pipit but the call is much deeper and the interval between each note is longer "chree ... chree ... chree".

DESCRIPTION: Because of its restricted range it is unlikely to be confused with any pipit other than the Grassveld, but it is **much more heavily streaked on the breast and has buffy outer tail feathers**. In addition the base of lower mandible is pink.

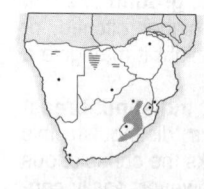

Yellow-breasted Pipit
Hemimacronyx chloris

illustrated page 27
(*Newman's Birds* p. 293)

HABITAT: Breeds in montane grassland above 1 400 m in South Africa. Unlike other pipits, it is not attracted to burnt ground or heavily grazed areas, and **prefers short, lush grassland which has not been disturbed for some time**. In the non-breeding season some birds move to lower altitudes where they can be found in pastures and even bushveld.

STATUS: Uncommon endemic resident.

BEHAVIOUR: Found mainly in pairs. Secretive and can be difficult to locate as it creeps through the grass. It flushes reluctantly, but then usually flies a long distance. The **distinctive call** is given either from a low perch such as an anthill, or in low, hovering flight.

CALL: A series of rapid chipping notes sounding like the call of a Long-tailed Widow "chip-chip-chip-chip-chip"; the song is a repetitive single "tseeu" or a double "see-chick ... see-chick ...", sometimes with the "tseeu" note added.

DESCRIPTION: During the breeding season this pipit has **bright yellow underparts which are very distinctive.** Unfortunately it usually settles with its back to the observer, and then looks much like a Grassveld Pipit which is a common species in the same habitat. When the bird flies the **yellow under-wing** coverts as well as the yellow underparts are obvious identification characters. In the non-breeding season it loses its yellow throat and breast, but still retains a **yellow patch on the belly** which is, however, not easy to see. It has a rather plain face (unlike the Grassveld Pipit) and shows no malar streak and very faint or no streaking on the breast.

Short-tailed Pipit
Anthus brachyurus

illustrated page 27
(*Newman's Birds* p. 287)

HABITAT: Moist grassland; it breeds in the higher, wet grassland in parts of KwaZulu-Natal and southern Mpumalanga and moves to coastal floodplains such as around St Lucia in the non-breeding season. It also has a restricted distribution on the floodplains in southern Mozambique.

STATUS: Uncommon resident.

BEHAVIOUR: Probably the most terrestrial of all pipits, it never perches in trees or bushes. A difficult species to flush, lifting out of the grass at the last minute, flying off in an erratic manner before dropping back into the grass some 20-30 m away, often running off in a crouched manner.

CALL: A nasal, buzzing "bzzht" given in flight or from the ground while perched on a small rock or termite mound.

DESCRIPTION: A **tiny** pipit. It is heavily marked on both upper- and underparts, and has a **short tail with clear white outer tail feathers.** In flight the tail is much thinner than that of other pipits. While habitat, markings and size help to distinguish it from most other pipits, it can easily be mistaken for a small female widow or a large cisticola, but the white outer tail feathers are characteristic.

Rocky hillsides

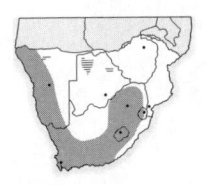

Long-billed Pipit
Anthus similis

illustrated page 27
(*Newman's Birds* p. 289)

HABITAT: Mainly rocky hillsides in grassland, particularly where the vegetation is rather sparse.

STATUS: Common resident.

BEHAVIOUR: Normally seen singly or in pairs. It is attracted to burnt areas and overgrazed lands alongside its rocky habitat. **It does not bob its tail like the very similar Grassveld Pipit.**

When disturbed will often fly up into a tree where it is quite at home.
CALL: It calls from rocks, shrubs and trees, often for extended periods, "tsip ... tsree ... trooop"; also a clear metallic "kilink" usually given when the bird flies up.
DESCRIPTION: It has a streaked back (more grey-brown than in the Grassveld Pipit) and a streaked breast. In the field almost identical to the Grassveld Pipit, but the **outer tail feathers are buff, not white**. This, combined with habitat and call, will help to separate the two species.

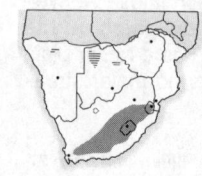

Rock Pipit
Anthus crenatus

illustrated page 27
(*Newman's Birds* p. 289)

HABITAT: Mountainous areas, ranging from high altitudes in Lesotho to koppies in the Karoo.
STATUS: Fairly common endemic resident.
BEHAVIOUR/CALL: Usually occurs singly or in pairs. Difficult to see and is mostly located by call. Has a characteristic stance when calling, **standing very erect with its bill pointing skywards**, usually on a rock or low bush. Sometimes calls in flight. The two-syllabled call "treee-terroooo" is repeated a number of times.
DESCRIPTION: Plain, with no streaking on the back and only very light streaking on the breast. The outer tail feathers are buff. It has a distinct buff eye-stripe which can be seen from a distance, but its other identification feature can only be seen at close range: yellow edges to the shoulder and flight feathers.

KAROO AND SEMI-ARID AREAS

Rock Pipit   *Anthus crenatus*
See above. Occurs in rocky areas in parts of the Karoo.

SUBURBIA

Plain-backed Pipit   *Anthus leucophrys*
See page 105. Visits gardens along the coast in areas such as Transkei.

• SEED-EATERS •

(This major group includes sparrows and brown canaries, and female and non-breeding weavers, bishops, widows, quelas, whydahs and widow finches.)

WOODLAND

Broad-leaved woodland

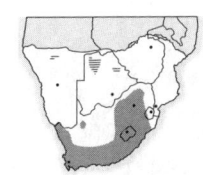

Cape Weaver — illustrated page 30
Ploceus capensis (*Newman's Birds* p. 409)
HABITAT: Most open habitats provided that there are a few trees with water nearby. Visits gardens.
STATUS: Common resident, endemic to South Africa.
BEHAVIOUR: Gregarious. It forages in small flocks on the ground or in trees. It nests colonially, preferably in a large tree, but will use reed-beds and even fences and telephone wires.
CALL: A swizzling sound, like that of the Spotted-backed Weaver, but lacking the final fade.
DESCRIPTION: This is one of the two **largest** weavers, about the size of a Golden Weaver. The top of the head is fairly flat, so that **in profile a near-straight line joins the tip of the bill to the top of the crown**. In non-breeding and female plumage the upperparts are dull olive, only slightly streaked, especially on the back; belly off-white, grading upwards to dull olive, tinged yellow in the breeding female. Bill is horn-coloured. Iris pale cream (adult male) or brown (female). Juvenile males have a brown iris which takes two years to turn cream. The legs are dull pink.

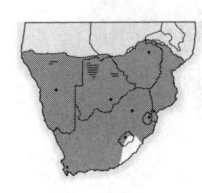

Masked Weaver — illustrated page 30
Ploceus velatus (*Newman's Birds* p. 413)
HABITAT: All habitats except evergreen forest and treeless desert; very partial to weedy and man-modified areas. The presence of water is not essential.
STATUS: Abundant resident.
BEHAVIOUR: Gregarious. Forages in flocks on the ground or in trees. It nests colonially in trees of any size, or in reed-beds.
CALL: A swizzle, very like that of the Cape Weaver.
DESCRIPTION: In non-breeding and female plumage the upperparts are dull streaky olive-brownish; belly white, grading upwards to buffish yellow. Bill horn. Iris red (adult males and breeding females) or brown (juveniles and most non-breeding females). The legs are dull pink.

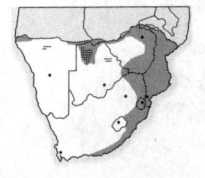

Spectacled Weaver — illustrated page 29
Ploceus ocularis (*Newman's Birds* p. 411)
HABITAT: Almost any wooded habitat except the interior of large forests.
STATUS: Common resident; territorial for much of the year.

110

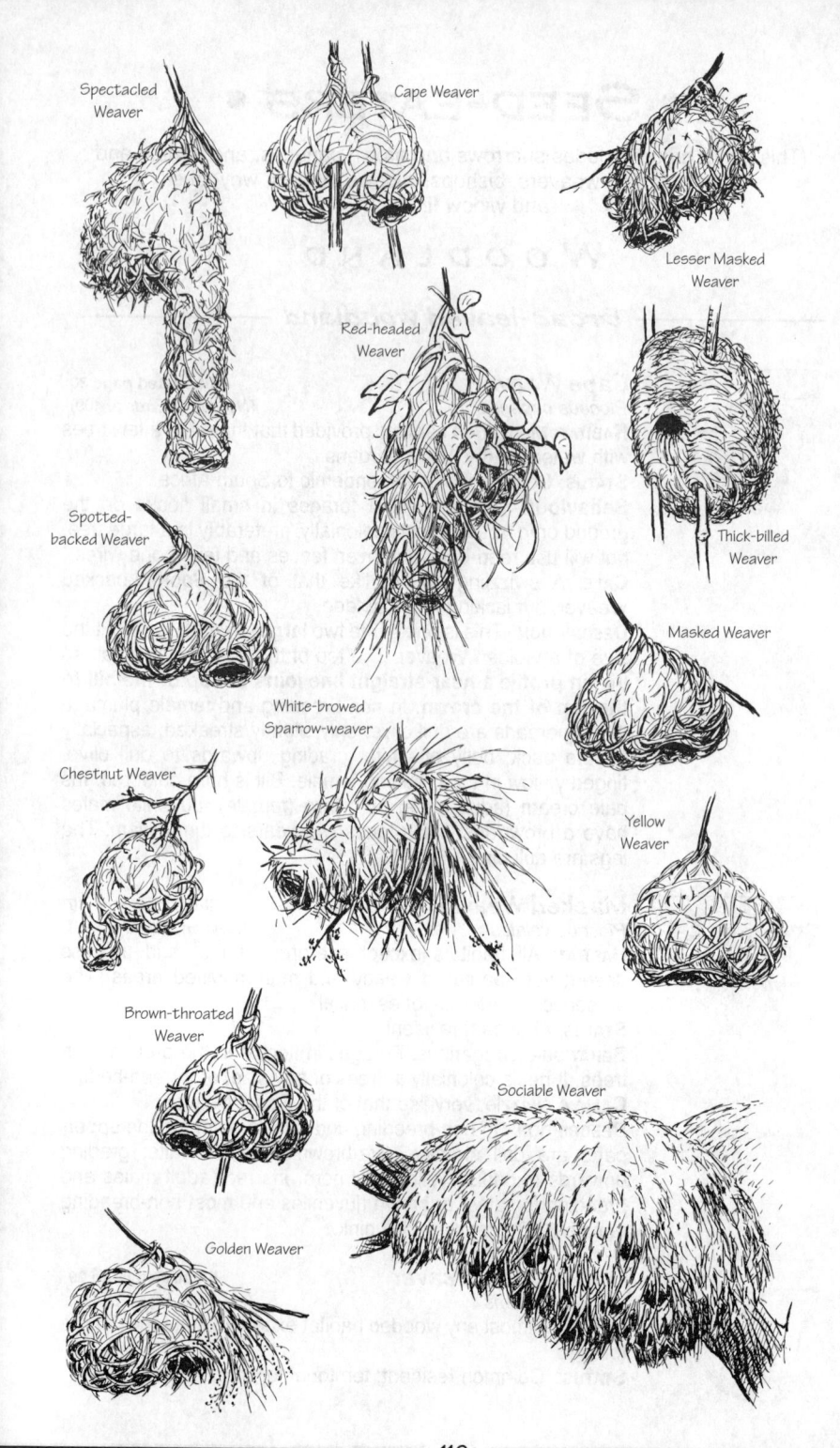

BEHAVIOUR: Behaves very much like the Forest Weaver but it makes extensive use of undergrowth, weedy thickets and woodland.
CALL: A descending series of short, clear, whistled notes.
DESCRIPTION: Predominantly a fairly uniform bright yellow throughout the year. **Both sexes have a narrow black streak through the eye,** and the male has, in addition, a black chin. The bill is black, the thinnest of all the weavers', and relatively long. Iris cream. Legs slate-grey. Juveniles lack the black facial features, have dull pinkish yellow bills and brown eyes. Adult colours develop at one year.

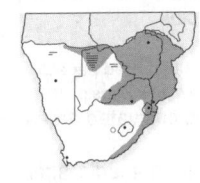

Spotted-backed Weaver
Ploceus cucullatus

illustrated page 30
(*Newman's Birds* p. 413)

HABITAT: Woodland, especially where large isolated trees overhang pans along riverine fringes; man-modified habitats, preferably near water.
STATUS: Abundant resident; locally nomadic during dry periods.
BEHAVIOUR: At all times gregarious. Food is picked from the ground, or when swinging in tall grass or in low bushy growth. It nests in large colonies and forages in flocks.
CALL: A harsh swizzling, fading away towards the end.
DESCRIPTION: Larger than most other weavers. In non-breeding and female plumage the **head is dull olive grading into a mottled greyish back** (diagnostic); the lower belly is white, grading into dull yellow upwards. Bill black (some adult males), or horn. Iris red (adult males and some females), or brown (subadults and some females). Legs dull pink.

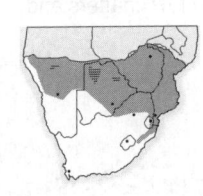

Lesser Masked Weaver
Ploceus intermedius

illustrated page 30
(*Newman's Birds* p. 413)

HABITAT: Riverine forest, woodland and reed-beds; occasionally suburbia.
STATUS: Locally abundant resident.
BEHAVIOUR: Always gregarious. Forages in small flocks in trees, rarely on the ground. It nests in trees or reed-beds, occasionally on buildings.
CALL: A harsh swizzle.
DESCRIPTION: This is **one of the smallest weavers**. In non-breeding and female plumage the upperparts are yellowish olive, lightly streaked; generally brighter than similar species; underparts are yellow (breeding females) or with belly white (non-breeders). Bill horn. Iris cream (adult males) or brown; subadult males show gradation in iris colour. The **legs are slate-grey**.

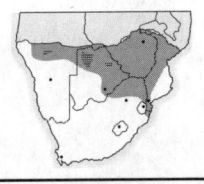

Red-headed Weaver
Anaplectes rubriceps

illustrated page 30
(*Newman's Birds* p. 413)

HABITAT: All woodland types; occasionally man-modified habitats.

STATUS: Locally common resident, but patchily distributed.
BEHAVIOUR: It forages singly or in a mixed bird party, behaving like a warbler or woodpecker in trees, inspecting leaves and bark, looking for insects. The nesting colonies – up to 10 nests – are sometimes in the same tree as colonies of buffalo weaver or sparrow-weaver nests. It may also nest solitarily.
CALL: A tuneless chatter, not a continuous swizzle like most other weavers.
DESCRIPTION: Small and delicately built. In non-breeding and female plumage the **head is dull orange**, grading towards olive down the back; the throat and breast are dull pale yellow, the belly is white. The bill is thin by weaver standards and pale red. The eye is red-brown, the legs are dull pink.

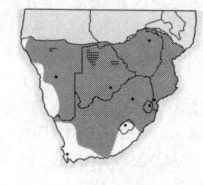

Red-billed Quelea
Quelea quelea

illustrated page 28
(*Newman's Birds* p. 405)

HABITAT: Woodland, grassland, reed-beds and cultivated areas provided that water is not too far distant.
STATUS: Common resident but may be highly nomadic after good rain.
BEHAVIOUR: **Very gregarious, flocks numbering millions at times**. Sometimes regarded as an agricultural pest. **Flocks have a characteristic "rolling" motion when foraging**, birds at the rear leap-frogging to get to the front. Forages for seeds on the ground, or may strip seeds from standing grasses. **Flying flocks swirl like smoke, so coordinated is the flight of individuals**. Non-breeding flocks roost tightly packed in a reed-bed or large tree.
CALL: Usually silent when foraging; at most a few chatters and wheezes.

Flight pattern of Red-billed Quelea flock

DESCRIPTION: Body size is small, tail nearly as short as that of bishops. In non-breeding and female plumage the upperparts are mottled greyish brown, notably greyer than any widow or bishop, especially on the crown. The eyebrow stripe is off-white. The underparts are unstreaked, breast pale greyish, fading to an off-white belly. The bill is red (non-breeding adults), dull yellow (breeding females) or pale horn (juveniles). The legs are pinker than those of bishops or widows.

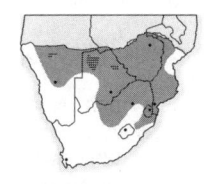

Paradise Whydah
Vidua paradisaea

illustrated page 31
(*Newman's Birds* p. 433)

HABITAT: Dry woodland and adjacent agricultural lands.
STATUS: Common resident, occasionally nomadic when not breeding.
BEHAVIOUR: Gregarious. It forms flocks of up to 100, both in and out of the breeding season. Forages by hopping forward and scratching the ground, favouring bare spots. The Melba Finch is the only known brood host.
CALL: A variety of chirps and tweeting notes, as well as imitations of the Melba Finch.
DESCRIPTION: The size of a sparrow, definitely larger than the Pin-tailed and Shaft-tailed Whydahs. Above, the female's plumage is scaled buff on dull grey, the rump being plain brownish grey. The crown is boldly streaked off-white and dark grey. The underparts are off-white, washed buff across the breast, with a few faint streaks on the throat. The bill is black, with a hint of red; the legs are pinkish brown. Non-breeding males are slightly brighter than the females. Males spend a long period in a transition dress: a patchwork black-and-white head and throat, a rusty breast and a dark-streaked rusty back.

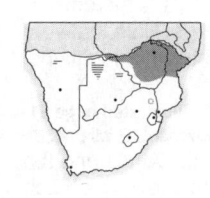

Broad-tailed Paradise Whydah
Vidua obtusa   (*Newman's Birds* p. 435)
HABITAT: Tall woodland.
STATUS: Uncommon resident; partially nomadic.
BEHAVIOUR: Gregarious, although is not normally found in large flocks. Forages on the ground in much the same style as other whydahs: hopping forward and scratching the ground as it lands, and inspecting its handiwork. It often mixes with the Golden-backed Pytilia, its brood host.
CALL: A series of twitters and cheeps, as well as imitations of the Golden-backed Pytilia.
DESCRIPTION: Sparrow-sized, much the same as the Paradise Whydah. Female plumage is similar to that of the Paradise Whydah, but differs in that the back is paler and less streaked; the rump is pale buff-grey; the crown stripes are less contrasting; the throat and breast are pastel grey with a few streaks, grading to pale buff-grey on the belly. The bill is horn-coloured; the legs are grey-brown.

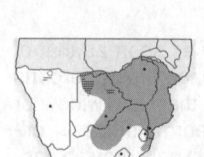

Steel-blue Widow Finch
Vidua chalybeata

illustrated page 31
(*Newman's Birds* p. 435)

HABITAT: Wooded country, including thickets and agricultural mosaics, but excluding forests.
STATUS: Common resident; nomadic at times.
BEHAVIOUR: Gregarious when not breeding, sometimes associating with the Red-billed Firefinch, its brood host. Forages for fallen seeds on the ground in the typical widow finch fashion: hopping forward and scratching the ground as it lands, and inspecting its handiwork.
CALL: A series of clear musical tweet notes, and imitations of the Red-billed Firefinch.
DESCRIPTION: Small: slightly smaller than any whydah. Non-breeding and female plumage is grey-brown above, scaled buff. The head stripes are brown and buff, but not clearly delineated as in other widow finches. The underparts are greyish buff, paling to an off-white belly. **The bill and legs are deep pink to red**: diagnostic.

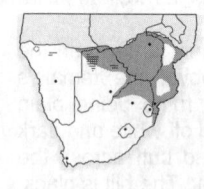

Purple Widow Finch
Vidua purpurascens

illustrated page 31
(*Newman's Birds* p. 435)

HABITAT: Most types of woodland; rarely in man-modified habitats. Until recently it was considered uncommon, but this may just be because it is difficult to recognise.
STATUS: Fairly common resident; probably nomadic.
BEHAVIOUR/CALL: Very few field notes about its behaviour exist. Calls include a variety of rapid ticks, some tweety notes, and imitations of Jameson's Firefinch, its brood host.
DESCRIPTION: Small: slightly smaller than any whydah. Non-breeding and female plumage is virtually identical to that of the Black Widow Finch. The best identifying feature is the **combination of a white bill and very pale pink legs**. Note that very few birds have white legs, as is often suggested in illustrations.

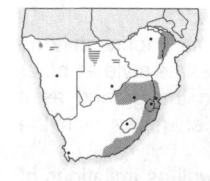

Black Widow Finch
Vidua funerea

illustrated page 31
(*Newman's Birds* p. 435)

HABITAT: Confined to the eastern part of South Africa and the eastern highlands of Zimbabwe. Older maps showing a much wider distribution are based upon misidentifications. It is found in a wide range of habitats, but most often on habitat boundaries where there is damp rank growth.
STATUS: Common resident; locally nomadic in winter.
BEHAVIOUR: Gregarious in winter. It normally forages on the ground, but is adapting to feeding tables. Winter flocks often mix with Blue-billed Firefinches, the brood host.
CALL: A rapid series of metallic notes, similar to but harsher than in the Blue-billed Firefinch.
DESCRIPTION: Small: slightly smaller than any whydah. Non-breeding and female plumage is grey-brown above, scaled

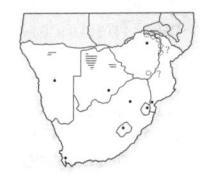

buff; the head stripes are dark grey and off-white. The underparts are pale buff, darker and greyer across the breast. The **white bill and bright pinkish red legs are diagnostic.**

Green Widow Finch
Vidua codringtoni   illustrated page 31
    (*Newman's Birds* p. 435)
HABITAT: Confined to thickets, woodland and forest edges in eastern and northern Zimbabwe. Has also been recorded near Harare, Kwekwe and Gwayi.
STATUS: Poorly known, but likely to be an uncommon resident.
BEHAVIOUR/CALL: Very few field notes exist. The call includes mimicry of the Red-throated Twinspot, its presumed brood host.
DESCRIPTION: Small: slightly smaller (but not diagnostically so) than other widow finches. Non-breeding and female plumage is very similar to that of other widow finches except for the greater contrast between the greyish breast and white belly. The **bill is white, the legs dull red, tending towards orange** rather than pink.

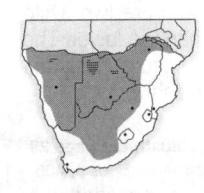

White-browed Sparrow-weaver
Plocepasser mahali   illustrated page 28
    (*Newman's Birds* p. 407)
HABITAT: Sparse woodland, man-modified habitats where grassland intersperses with scattered trees, and particularly areas where bare ground is adjacent to fairly thick grass.
STATUS: Common resident.
BEHAVIOUR: Gregarious. Typically found in **small flocks of about six**; these birds are usually closely related and constitute a cooperative breeding unit. Flocks forage on bare ground where the birds are quite mobile and move around constantly. If disturbed, the flock flies into a nearby tree. The birds rarely move far from the nesting tree, which can easily be identified by the untidy grass-ball nests.
CALL: A series of musical chirpy notes.
DESCRIPTION: A chunky bird, about the size of a large weaver. Above, the plumage is brown, except for a white rump, white eyebrow stripe and white edges to the wing feathers; the cheeks are almost black. The underparts are white; the legs dull brown. The only sexual difference is apparent in the bill: **males have a black bill, females a horn-coloured bill.**

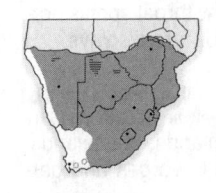

Southern Grey-headed Sparrow
Passer diffusus   illustrated page 29
    (*Newman's Birds* p. 405)
HABITAT: Almost any wooded habitat except forest; has adapted to man-modified habitats.
STATUS: Common resident.
BEHAVIOUR: Normally found singly or in pairs; small flocks may form in winter. It nearly always forages on the ground, walking slowly as it looks for food.

CALL: A series of shrill chipping notes, all slightly different but of similar pitch.
DESCRIPTION: The sexes are alike. The head is plain pale grey, the rest of the upperparts, particularly the rump, being rufous. There is **only one, very bold white wing-bar**. The underparts are very pale grey, almost white.

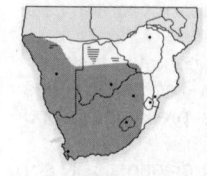

Cape Sparrow
Passer melanurus

illustrated page 29
(*Newman's Birds* p. 407)

HABITAT: Sparsely wooded areas, including semi-desert and man-modified habitats.
STATUS: Common resident; occasionally nomadic.
BEHAVIOUR: In summer it is usually seen in pairs, but large flocks may form in winter. Forages by hopping on the ground.
CALL: Quite musical, certainly by sparrow standards: a variable series of whistled cheeps.
DESCRIPTION: Males are much more brightly coloured than females: the head, face and throat are black, with a bold white crescent behind the cheek. The rest of the upperparts, especially the rump, are mainly a rich brown. There are two white bars on the wing, the upper being brighter than the lower. The underparts are white. The female is a more muted version, differing most notably in that the facial mask is light grey.

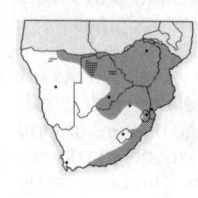

Yellow-throated Sparrow
Petronia superciliaris

illustrated page 29
(*Newman's Birds* p. 405)

HABITAT: All wooded habitats except forests, provided that there is little or no undergrowth.
STATUS: Fairly common resident.
BEHAVIOUR: Normally seen singly or in pairs, walking on bare ground looking for fallen seeds or insects. Otherwise it may forage in woody vegetation in the manner of a warbler. **Typically flicks its tail upon landing.**
CALL: Distinctive: three evenly spaced, descending chipping notes.
DESCRIPTION: The sexes are alike. The upperparts are dull brown with a few darker streaks on the back. The head is plain brown with a **bold off-white eyebrow stripe that extends to the back of the head**. There are two pale bars on the wing, the upper being bolder than the lower. The underparts are dull pale grey except for a white chin. The yellow throat spot is normally invisible; presumably it is reserved for rare displays.

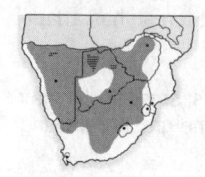

Black-throated Canary
Serinus atrogularis

illustrated page 31
(*Newman's Birds* p. 439)

HABITAT: Woodland, savanna, fallow farmlands, wastelands, riparian bush in semi-arid regions, roadside verges and gardens; seldom far from water.
STATUS: Common resident in the highveld and semi-arid west.

BEHAVIOUR: Small flocks can sometimes be seen feeding on the seed-heads of grasses.
CALL: A sweet "twee" with rising intonation. It also sings a **sustained jumble of pleasant trills delivered in hurried sequence.**
DESCRIPTION: Smaller than a House Sparrow. Sexes are alike. Usually has a diagnostic **black throat patch**; this is sometimes reduced to a few black speckles. In flight shows a **bright yellow rump.** (The only other brown canary with a yellow rump is the larger White-throated Canary, which has a white throat.)

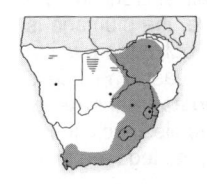

Streaky-headed Canary   illustrated page 31
Serinus gularis   (*Newman's Birds* p. 439)
HABITAT: Savanna, open woodland, secondary growth around cultivations, riparian bush, bushy hillsides and gardens.
STATUS: Common resident; largely nomadic.
BEHAVIOUR: Quiet and unobtrusive when not singing. Forages on the ground, in bushes and in trees. Sings from the top of a tall tree.
CALL: A three-syllabled "chirririt" call. In summer it sings a loud and clear jumble of musical notes in **short strophes of about three seconds' duration.**
DESCRIPTION: Sparrow-sized and sparrow-like. The sexes are alike, with **prominent white eyebrows**, heavy conical bill and the **top of the head streaked black and white.** (The Yellow-throated Sparrow also has white eyebrows, but has white wing-bars, no head streaks and a less heavy bill.)

Yellow Weaver   *Ploceus subaureus*
See page 120.

Thornveld

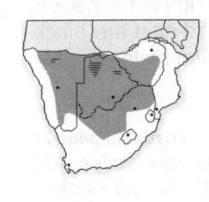

Shaft-tailed Whydah   illustrated page 31
Vidua regia   (*Newman's Birds* p. 433)
HABITAT: Dry thornveld and adjacent agricultural lands.
STATUS: Common resident; may be nomadic when not breeding.
BEHAVIOUR: Most often seen in small flocks foraging on the ground, scratching around for seeds. Polygamous in the breeding season, with juveniles often attending a male and his females. The Violet-eared Waxbill is the brood host.
CALL: A hoarse wheeze, sometimes including imitations of the Violet-eared Waxbill.
DESCRIPTION: Non-breeding and female plumage is a warm brown above, streaked darker brown. The underparts are off-white, buffier on the throat and breast. The bill and legs are a fairly bright red.

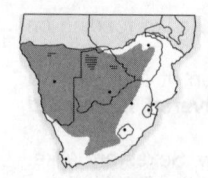

Scaly-feathered Finch
Sporopipes squamifrons

illustrated page 28
(*Newman's Birds* p. 407)

Habitat: Sparse woodland **with grasses**; absent from grassless areas. Occasionally gardens and farmyards.
Status: Abundant resident; nomadic in response to localised crops of grass seeds.
Behaviour: It always forms small flocks, and is usually seen foraging on the ground. If disturbed, the whole flock takes refuge in the nearest bush.
Call: A pleasant, varied series of cheeping notes.
Description: Small, about the size of the smallest firefinch. The build is compact. The sexes are alike. Above, the plumage is dull brown, the wing feathers being darker but edged white. The underparts are pale buff, darker on the breast. The face is elegantly marked with black: **two broad moustachial streaks and neat mottling on the forehead.** Juveniles lack these black marks. The bill is conical and dull pink; the legs are pinkish brown.

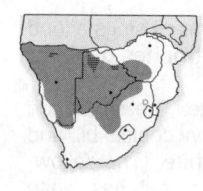

Great Sparrow
Passer motitensis

illustrated page 29
(*Newman's Birds* p. 407)

Habitat: Confined to dry woodland and scrub in the dry northwest, but excluding the very driest areas and the Okavango.
Status: Uncommon resident.
Behaviour: Typically occurs in pairs. It is **retiring in nature, and never associated with human settlements**. Usually seen foraging for seeds and insects on the ground, or visiting waterholes.
Call: Chipping notes.
Description: Slightly larger than the House Sparrow. It is sexually dimorphic, but less markedly so than the House Sparrow. The upperparts of the male are brown, lightly streaked black; rump rufous brown. The white wing-bar is longer than that of the House Sparrow. The crown and nape are pale grey, the grey extending in a narrow band around the side of the neck to join the white underparts. The eye-stripe and chin are black. The female is a paler and duller version of the male, and has no black on the face or chin.

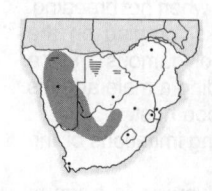

Sociable Weaver
Philetairus socius

illustrated page 28
(*Newman's Birds* p. 407)

Habitat: Woodland, which must include both *Acacia erioloba* for **nesting trees and certain stiff grasses for nest construction,** ranging from northern Namibia to the north-western interior of South Africa.
Status: Abundant endemic resident.
Behaviour: Gregarious and, unusually for a species of dry areas, very sedentary. Individuals rarely move far from their haystack-like communal nest. Forages in flocks on bare

ground, scratching around with the bill rather than the feet. Sociable Weavers are always adding to their nest, and may be found carrying pieces of grass at any time of year.
CALL: A rapid series of chipping notes, not unmusical.
DESCRIPTION: Fairly small, slightly smaller than a sparrow. The sexes are alike. The upperparts are greyish brown, plain on the crown and rump, neatly scaled pale buff on the back and wings. The underparts are pale buff except for a small patch on the flank where the feathers are black, edged white. The face and chin are black. The legs and bill are light grey. Juveniles lack the black face and flanks, and have light brown legs and bills.

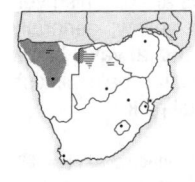

Chestnut Weaver   illustrated page 29
Ploceus rubiginosus   (*Newman's Birds* p. 409)
HABITAT: Thornveld and sparsely wooded grassland in central and northern Namibia.
STATUS: Locally common resident; semi-nomadic depending on rainfall.
BEHAVIOUR: Always gregarious, nesting colonially and foraging in flocks on or near the ground. Its food is scarcely known but, judging from bill design, presumably consists mostly of seeds.
CALL: A series of chatters and cheeps.
DESCRIPTION: Females and non-breeding males look more like female widows than weavers. The head is greyish olive with darker streaks and a yellowish eyebrow; the back is streaky brownish grey; underparts off-white with a brown tinge to the breast. Generally browner than most widows. Bill horn, eyes brown, legs pale grey.

Black Widow Finch   *Vidua funerea*
See page 114.

Masked Weaver   *Ploceus velatus*
See page 109.

Red-billed Quelea   *Quelea quelea*
See page 112.

Red-collared Widow   *Euplectes ardens*
See page 123.

White-browed Sparrow-weaver   *Plocepasser mahali*
See page 115.

White-winged Widow   *Euplectes albonotatus*
See page 123.

Grassland and Marshland

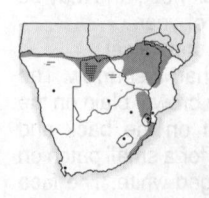

Golden Weaver
Ploceus xanthops

illustrated page 29
(*Newman's Birds* p. 411)

Habitat: Rank waterside vegetation and forest edges.
Status: Uncommon resident.
Behaviour: A **solitary nester beside water**. It forages singly or in small groups in long grass, bushes and trees. This is a furtive bird, not easily seen.
Call: A continuous swizzling.
Description: Large, about the size of a Cape Weaver, from which it is easily distinguished by the **markedly rounded head** and the obviously longer tail. The upperparts are greenish yellow with no streaking; underparts uniform yellow; generally brighter than similar species. **Bill heavy and always black** (adults); juveniles have horn-coloured bills. Iris pale pinkish yellow (adults) or brown (juveniles). Legs dull pink.

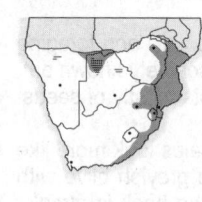

Thick-billed Weaver
Amblyospiza albifrons

illustrated page 29
(*Newman's Birds* p. 411)

Habitat: Reed-beds in summer, evergreen forests and weed infestations in winter.
Status: Common resident.
Behaviour: Gregarious at all times. It forages in flocks, often in the forest canopy, commuting long distances to reach favourite fruiting trees. It breeds colonially in reed-beds.
Call: A pleasant twittering, most often heard from flocks flying overhead to feeding grounds.
Description: Large. In female and juvenile plumage the upperparts are mottled light brown; underparts off-white, heavily mottled brown on the throat and breast, less so on the belly. **The bill is heavy and triangular; straw-yellow (adult females)**, dark horn (subadults) tending to black (males approaching breeding age). The eye is brown, the legs dark grey. Adult males have an eclipse plumage identical to the uniformly dark brown breeding dress except that the white patches on the head are lost.

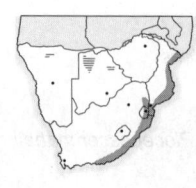

Yellow Weaver
Ploceus subaureus

illustrated page 29
(*Newman's Birds* p. 411)

Habitat: Reed-beds and woodland, occasionally evergreen forest.
Status: Common resident.
Behaviour: Always gregarious. Forages in flocks on the ground and in trees. Nests colonially, usually in reed-beds, sometimes in adjacent trees.
Call: A swizzle, typically faster than most other weavers.
Description: The head is rounded. The upperparts are dull olive, lightly streaked. The underparts are pale bright yellow

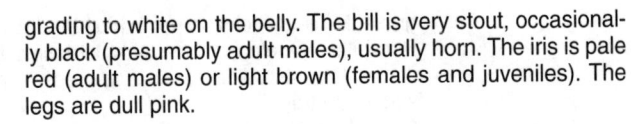

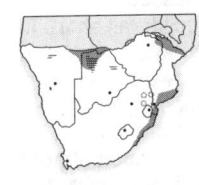

grading to white on the belly. The bill is very stout, occasionally black (presumably adult males), usually horn. The iris is pale red (adult males) or light brown (females and juveniles). The legs are dull pink.

Brown-throated Weaver
Ploceus xanthopterus

illustrated page 29
(*Newman's Birds* p. 411)

HABITAT: Reed-beds and other dense vegetation beside water.
STATUS: Uncommon, localised resident.
BEHAVIOUR: Always gregarious. It forages in waterside vegetation and breeds in small colonies in reed-beds, often amid a larger colony of Yellow Weavers.
CALL: A diverse array of notes, scarcely musical, but more tuneful than the calls of most weavers.
DESCRIPTION: Small. The head is squarish when compared with those of other weavers. In non-breeding and female plumage the upperparts are dull olive, washed **cinnamon** on the rump. The underparts are dull yellow grading to white on the belly. The bill is stout and horn-coloured. Iris brown; legs pink.

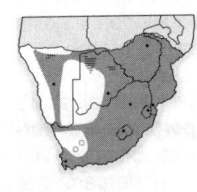

Pin-tailed Whydah
Vidua macroura

illustrated page 31
(*Newman's Birds* p. 433)

HABITAT: A variety of habitats: grassland, wetland, sparse woodland and almost any man-modified habitat.
STATUS: Common resident; may be nomadic when not breeding.
BEHAVIOUR: **Polygamous in the breeding season**, with up to six females attending the male, hence its nickname "king-of-six". It forms small flocks in winter, foraging for seeds on open ground or dominating a bird table. It parasitises the Common Waxbill, occasionally the Bronze Mannikin or other small species.
CALL: A pleasant series of jerky disconnected notes.
DESCRIPTION: In non-breeding and female plumage the upperparts are dark brownish grey scaled bright buff. The head is boldly striped rufous-buff and black. The breast is light buff, paling to off-white on the belly. Legs dark grey; bill dull red.

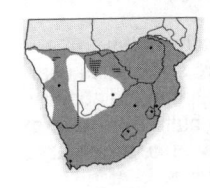

Red Bishop
Euplectes orix

illustrated page 30
(*Newman's Birds* p. 417)

HABITAT: Most open habitats **provided water is nearby**: marshes, reed-beds, grassland, cultivated fields and gardens. Occurs virtually throughout southern Africa except in the waterless parts of the Namib and Kalahari.
STATUS: Abundant resident.
BEHAVIOUR: Gregarious at all times. Forages in flocks, sometimes numbering thousands, nearly always on the ground picking up fallen seeds. It occasionally strips seeds from standing

grass. Moving flocks do not exhibit the "rolling" action typical of Red-billed Queleas – the only lookalike forming such large flocks. It nests colonially in long grass or reed-beds, rarely in waterside trees.
CALL: A harsh array of rattles, wheezes and hisses.
DESCRIPTION: Characteristically compact of build; tail short. In non-breeding and female plumage the upperparts are mottled greyish brown (adults), or obviously yellower, less grey (recently fledged juveniles). The eyebrow stripe is dull yellowish white. The underparts are pale buff, throat and upper breast streaked brown. **The under-tail coverts reach almost to the notch in the tail, a feature shared only with the Golden Bishop.**

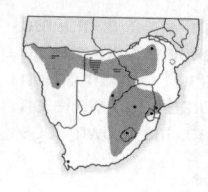

Golden Bishop
Euplectes afer
illustrated page 30
(*Newman's Birds* p. 417)

HABITAT: Vleis, surrounding weedy thickets and damp grassland.
STATUS: Locally common resident.
BEHAVIOUR: Gregarious at all times. Forages in flocks of up to 100, often with other bishops and widows, picking seeds off the ground or stripping them from standing vegetation. It nests in small colonies in reed-beds or adjacent low vegetation.
CALL: A high-pitched, rasping series of squeaks.
DESCRIPTION: Body size is small, build compact and tail short. In non-breeding and female plumage the **upperparts are mottled blackish brown** (darker than in the Red Bishop). The eyebrow stripe is pale yellowish white. The underparts are nearly white, streaked brown on throat and breast, although less boldly so than in the Red Bishop. The under-tail coverts reach almost to the notch in the tail, a feature shared only with the Red Bishop.

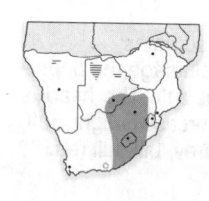

Long-tailed Widow
Euplectes progne
illustrated page 31
(*Newman's Birds* p. 419)

HABITAT: Open grassland and vleis.
STATUS: Common resident; semi-nomadic in winter.
BEHAVIOUR: Always gregarious, and especially when not breeding may form large flocks. It forages on the ground for seeds and insects.
CALL: Normally silent; may utter a few scratchy notes.
DESCRIPTION: The size is variable, males are sometimes nearly twice the body weight of females. Female plumage above is mottled greyish brown, the eyebrow stripe buff. The **bend of the wing often – but by no means always – has a coloured patch**. In females and first-year males this is faint rusty or absent; second-year males have a mottled dark chestnut patch; adult eclipse males have a solid orange patch fringed pale brown. Adult males also have black primaries. The under-

parts are pale brownish buff – no orange or rusty tinges. The **breast is always streaked, sometimes quite boldly, and streaking may extend to the throat.**

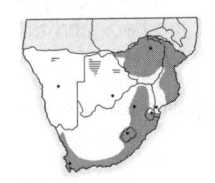

Yellow-rumped Widow
Euplectes capensis

illustrated page 31
(*Newman's Birds* p. 419)

HABITAT: Damp valleys with rank vegetation along drainage lines; normally avoids vleis and open water.
STATUS: Locally common resident; somewhat nomadic in winter.
BEHAVIOUR: Gregarious. Forages in small flocks on bare ground or in rank vegetation. Breeds in small colonies.
CALL: Weedy cheep notes; in display it utters regular high-pitched wheezes.
DESCRIPTION: Non-breeding and female plumage is mottled greyish brown above with a buff eyebrow stripe. **The rump is washed mustard-yellow.** The **bend of the wing has a mottled mustard patch** (females and juveniles) or a plain yellow patch (non-breeding adult males). Underparts buff, paling towards the belly, with heavy streaking (broader streaks than in bishops) on the throat and breast.

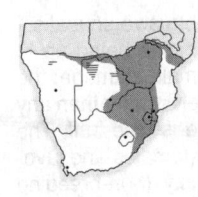

White-winged Widow
Euplectes albonotatus

illustrated page 30
(*Newman's Birds* p. 417)

HABITAT: Rank vegetation, weedy thickets, cultivated lands and thornveld, not necessarily near water, in the east and northeast. It avoids the Kalahari and southern highveld.
STATUS: Common resident; locally abundant.
BEHAVIOUR: Always gregarious, although **females are not usually conspicuous when breeding.** Forms flocks in winter, feeding mainly on bare ground, sometimes on standing grass.
CALL: Mostly silent; some unobtrusive scratches and twitters.
DESCRIPTION: Slender build compared with other widows and bishops. Non-breeding and female plumage is mottled greyish brown above, the eyebrow stripe dull yellow. The bend of the wing is mottled mustard-yellow (females and juveniles), or solid yellow with a broad white fringe (non-breeding adult males). Adult males always have black primaries. The underparts are pale yellow-buff, the yellow wash being more apparent about the chin and the upper breast in adult males; sides of breast slightly streaked.

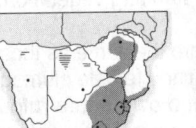

Red-collared Widow
Euplectes ardens

illustrated page 30
(*Newman's Birds* p. 417)

HABITAT: Grassland, sparse thornveld, edges of vleis and cultivation, mainly in the eastern third of southern Africa.
STATUS: Common resident; semi-nomadic in winter.
BEHAVIOUR: Always gregarious, most obviously when not breeding. Forms flocks, often mixing with other widows and bishops. It usually forages on the ground.

CALL: A rapid series of high-pitched hisses.
DESCRIPTION: The build is slender. Female plumage is mottled greyish brown above, slightly but definitely darker than other widows and bishops, especially on the crown. Adult males in eclipse plumage have black primaries and the back and tail feathers are black, broadly edged buff. The eyebrow stripe is buff with a hint of orange. The underparts are entirely without streaks; the breast is light orange-brown, paling towards the throat and belly.

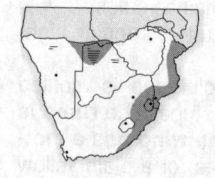

Red-shouldered Widow
Euplectes axillaris

illustrated page 30
(*Newman's Birds* p. 417)

HABITAT: Any completely **open habitat provided water is nearby**: grassland, vleis, fringes of cultivation.
STATUS: Abundant resident; some local movements away from breeding grounds in winter.
BEHAVIOUR: Nearly always gregarious. Comparatively unobtrusive in the breeding season but forms huge flocks in winter. Birds forage for seeds on open ground, often mixing with other widows and bishops.
CALL: Not very vocal; utters a series of unobtrusive squeaks.
DESCRIPTION: Body size is variable, some males being up to twice the body weight of small females. Female plumage: the upperparts are mottled greyish rusty (definitely redder than any other widow or bishop). The eyebrow stripe is pale buff. The bend of the wing has a mottled rusty patch (females and juveniles) or a bright orange patch fringed rusty (non-breeding adult males). Adult males always have black primaries. The underparts are pale rusty buff with a few streaks at the side of the breast; **under-wing coverts rusty, obvious in flight**.

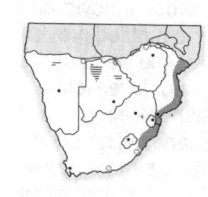

Red-headed Quelea
Quelea erythrops

(*Newman's Birds* p. 403)

HABITAT: Wetland, reed-beds and the thick weedy vegetation surrounding them.
STATUS: Uncommon summer-breeding migrant; a few individuals overwinter. Not as rare as formerly supposed.
BEHAVIOUR: Always gregarious. Forages in small flocks, or mixes with larger flocks of bishops and widows. Forages for seeds on the ground, or more usually in standing vegetation.
CALL: A few quiet chattering notes.
DESCRIPTION: Body size and proportions are the same as those of the Red-billed Quelea. In non-breeding and female plumage the upperparts are mottled dark and light brown with a rufous tinge. The crown is mottled brownish orange. The eyebrow stripe is pale dull orange, and the whole face has an orange blush. Underparts are unstreaked, off-white with an orange-brown tinge.

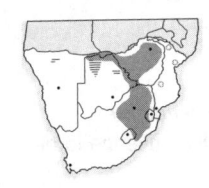

Cuckoo Finch
Anomalospiza imberbis

illustrated page 31
(*Newman's Birds* p. 431)

HABITAT: Primarily grassland but also sparse woodland, wetland and cultivated areas.
STATUS: Uncommon resident.
BEHAVIOUR: Usually solitary or in pairs. It forages for seeds on standing vegetation.
CALL: A series of rasping notes.
DESCRIPTION: In appearance this bird is not unlike a female Red Bishop. It has a **compact build and is notably deep-chested**. The sexes are alike. The plumage above is mottled buff and greyish brown, the "scaling" effect being generally finer than in a bishop. The eyebrow stripe is indistinct. The throat and breast are finely streaked brownish on buff. Streaking extends to the belly, getting fainter, the belly itself being very pale buff. The legs are brownish grey, darker than those of a bishop. The bill is dark horn and conical, shorter in proportion than that of a bishop.

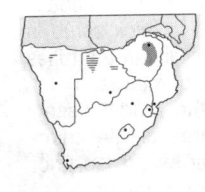

Yellow-backed Widow
Euplectes macrourus

illustrated page 30
(*Newman's Birds* p. 419)

HABITAT: Vleis, moist grassland and man-modified bare areas. Virtually confined to the Mashonaland Plateau of Zimbabwe.
STATUS: Fairly common resident.
BEHAVIOUR: Always gregarious; most obviously so when not breeding. Forages in small flocks on the ground and in short dense vegetation. Often mixes with other widows and bishops.
CALL: A few thin, high-pitched notes.
DESCRIPTION: Female plumage is mottled greyish brown above with a pale buff eyebrow stripe. Adult non-breeding males have black primaries and a yellow patch on the bend of the wing. The underparts are pale buff, with light streaking on the breast only. The tail is slightly but obviously longer than those of most other widows.

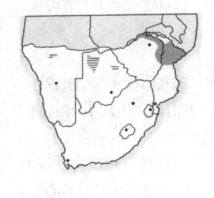

Fire-crowned Bishop
Euplectes hordeaceus

illustrated page 30
(*Newman's Birds* p. 417)

HABITAT: Rank vegetation in and beside vleis and streams. Confined to northern and eastern Zimbabwe and Mozambique.
STATUS: Uncommon, localised resident.
BEHAVIOUR: Usually gregarious, but never seen in large numbers. Forages on the ground or in low vegetation, taking mostly seeds. It breeds in reed-beds or long grass.
CALL: Very similar to that of the Red Bishop.
DESCRIPTION: Very similar in every way to the Red Bishop, **except that the primary wing feathers and tail are blackish**.

Cape Weaver   *Ploceus capensis*
See page 109.

Lark-like Bunting *Emberiza impetuani*
See opposite.

Lesser Masked Weaver *Ploceus intermedius*
See page 111. Occurs in reed-beds as well as riverine forest and woodland.

Red-billed Quelea *Quelea quelea*
See page 112.

FYNBOS

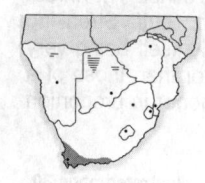

Protea Canary   illustrated page 31
Serinus leucopterus   (Newman's Birds p. 439)
HABITAT: Confined to the protea belt of the Cape mountains; also wooded kloofs in the area.
STATUS: Uncommon resident, endemic to South Africa.
BEHAVIOUR: Secretive, staying mostly in dense cover. Feeds in stands of proteas on mountain slopes, and in thick scrub in valleys, but sings from an exposed perch. If disturbed it flies away swiftly and directly for many hundreds of metres.
CALL: The call note is "tree, treareearee"; the sprightly song, delivered from the top of a bush, is "chiree chiree chiree chiree, tawit, tirrit tirrit tirrit tirrit, twit twit twit twit, trrioo trrioo trioo trioo ..." in strophes of about 10 seconds' duration.
DESCRIPTION: A large, grey-brown canary. Two white wing bars are an obvious diagnostic character when the bird is perched. The bill is very large and pale in colour. It has a white throat bar below a black chin.

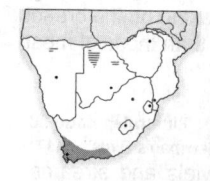

Cape Siskin   illustrated page 31
Pseudochloroptila totta   (Newman's Birds p. 441)
HABITAT: Confined to the mountains of the south-western Cape: fynbos-covered mountain slopes, old clear-felled timber plantations and forest fringes.
STATUS: Fairly common endemic resident.
BEHAVIOUR: Small flocks feed on the ground and in low bushes. May sometimes be seen on mountain paths, but flushes quickly and is not easily studied.
CALL: A weak, high-pitched "tchwing, tchwing", and "pitchee" at each dip of the undulating flight. Also has a rambling, high-pitched song with distinct "sweet-sweet, checer" sounds and frequent trills.
DESCRIPTION: Rich brown on the upperparts and dull yellow below, the female being more dusky about the breast. In flight shows **white tips to the primary feathers and tail**. Its range does not overlap with that of the Drakensberg Siskin.

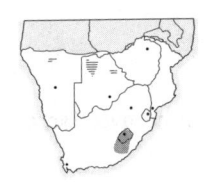

Drakensberg Siskin
Pseudochloroptila symonsi

illustrated page 31
(*Newman's Birds* p. 441)

HABITAT: High grassy slopes and scrubland of mountains in the north-eastern Cape, Lesotho and eastern Free State.
STATUS: Common endemic resident at very high altitudes.
BEHAVIOUR: Pairs and flocks feed mostly on the ground, among rocks or in bushes. Shy, but soon resettles if flushed.
CALL: The canary-like song is rapid and rambling, with "cher-twee, chit-chit-chit" sounds and trills.
DESCRIPTION: The male is similar to the male Cape Siskin but the female is entirely brown. In flight displays white outer tail feathers. Its range does not overlap with that of the Cape Siskin.

KAROO AND SEMI-ARID AREAS

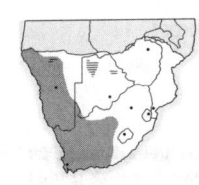

White-throated Canary
Serinus albogularis

illustrated page 31
(*Newman's Birds* p. 439)

HABITAT: Karoo thorn scrub in river valleys, dry scrub on hillsides, desert and coastal dunes in the southern Karoo and northwards through Namaqualand to Namibia. Seldom far from water.
STATUS: Common resident.
BEHAVIOUR: Singly or in small flocks, but mostly unobtrusive. Forages on the ground, where it hops; also in proteas.
CALL: A deep "squee-yik"; the song is a typical canary jumble of rolling whistles, churrs and chipperings with a loud nasal "skweer" frequently interspersed; it is hurried and delivered in short bursts.
DESCRIPTION: The sexes are alike. Ash-brown. Diagnostic features are the **white throat and greenish yellow rump**.

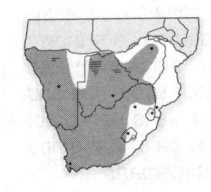

Lark-like Bunting
Emberiza impetuani

illustrated page 31
(*Newman's Birds* p. 443)

HABITAT: A variety of habitats including grassland, Karoo and semi-arid areas, often in rocky regions of the south-western semi-arid zone.
STATUS: Common to abundant resident; highly nomadic.
BEHAVIOUR: Gregarious; in flocks. In cold weather often erupts in the north or east in large numbers. Feeds on the ground or on grass heads.
CALL: The song is a rapidly delivered "trrrooo-cheeoo-cheepp-trree" repeated frequently.
DESCRIPTION: Small, cinnamon-washed, mostly lacking in diagnostic features. The sexes are alike.

FOREST

Forest Weaver   *Ploceus bicolor*
See page 84. This brightly coloured weaver behaves like a large warbler and feeds mainly on insects.

Golden Weaver   *Ploceus xanthops*
See page 120. Occurs in forest edges and rank waterside vegetation.

Green Widow Finch   *Vidua codringtoni*
See page 115. Occurs in forest edges.

Thick-billed Weaver   *Amblyospiza albifrons*
See page 120. Occurs in evergreen forest, particularly in winter.

Yellow Weaver   *Ploceus subaureus*
See page 120. Occasionally in evergreen forest.

SUBURBIA

House Sparrow   illustrated page 29
Passer domesticus   (*Newman's Birds* p. 405)

HABITAT: Confined to suburbia, villages and the fringes of major roads.
STATUS: Abundant resident. An alien species, introduced to Durban before 1900.
BEHAVIOUR: Pairs maintain very small territories. It usually hops around on bare ground looking for virtually anything edible. Is always checking crevices in buildings for potential nest sites.
CALL: A series of chipping notes.
DESCRIPTION: Shows clear **sexual dimorphism**; the male and female usually associate closely, making comparison easy. The male is quite brightly coloured: the upperparts are brown streaked black, except for the grey rump (diagnostic) and crown. The cheek is white, framed by a black eye-stripe and throat. The underparts are off-white. The female is very drab: the upperparts are dull light brown, with a pale buff stripe behind the eye. The wing-bar is faint. The underparts are off-white.

Black Widow Finch   *Vidua funerea*
See page 114.

Black-throated Canary   *Serinus atrogularis*
See page 116.

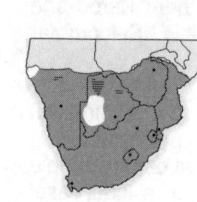

Seed-eaters

Cape Sparrow *Passer melanurus*
See page 116.

Cape Weaver *Ploceus capensis*
See page 109. Visits gardens.

Lesser Masked Weaver *Ploceus intermedius*
See page 111. Occasionally found in suburbia.

Masked Weaver *Ploceus velatus*
See page 109. Common in gardens. The presence of water is not essential.

Pin-tailed Whydah *Vidua macroura*
See page 121. Loves feeding tables with seeds and chases away most other birds around them.

Red Bishop *Euplectes orix*
See page 121. Occurs in gardens if water is nearby.

Scaly-feathered Finch *Sporopipes squamifrons*
See page 118.

Southern Grey-headed Sparrow *Passer diffusus*
See page 115. Has adapted to man-modified habitats.

Spectacled Weaver *Ploceus ocularis*
See page 109.

Spotted-backed Weaver *Ploceus cucullatus*
See page 111. Occurs in gardens, preferably near water.

Streaky-headed Canary *Serinus gularis*
See page 117.

• GLOSSARY •

acacia: deciduous trees of the genus *Acacia*. In Africa these are thorny, with bipinnately compound leaves (each leaf is again divided into small leaflets) and small, powderpuff-like or elongated flowers.

broad-leaved woodland: woodland comprised of trees with broad leaves as opposed to thornveld where trees of the genus *Acacia* are dominant.

bushveld: a terrain with mixed trees of moderate height (5-10 m) in which the trees frequently touch each other below canopy height; sometimes in dense thickets and usually with a grassy groundcover.

display: a term used to denote actions that have become ritualised in the course of evolution: threat display, courtship display, social displays, etc.

ecotone: the interface between different ecological regions; usually made up of components of each adjoining region.

edge: a non-technical synonym for ecotone. A transitional zone between two different types of habitat.

endemic: refers to species found only in a specific region or country.

escarpment: the long steep face of a plateau. In southern Africa usually refers to the eastern escarpment which forms the edge of the inland plateau or highveld.

fynbos: a natural habitat occurring in the south-eastern and south-western coastal regions of the Cape; a Mediterranean-type scrub composed of proteas, ericas and legumes among other plants.

jizz: the general impression of a bird – its family characteristics.

leaf-gleaner: a bird that pecks insects from the leaves of the tree canopy.

miombo: broad-leaved woodland in which trees of the genus *Brachystegia* dominate; common in Zimbabwe with small regions in north-eastern Botswana.

mistbelt: the eastern region of southern Africa at 900-1 350 m above sea-level (otherwise known as the escarpment) where the rainfall is between 900-1 150 mm per annum and the conditions are frequently misty during easterly maritime winds; of mostly hilly or montane grassland with isolated forest patches and, these days, with exotic plantations.

montane: mountainous country.

mopane: a broad-leaved, deciduous tree, *Colophospermum mopane*, found in much of the north and north-east of Botswana. May grow to a height of about 10 m, the leaves rounded, heart-shaped and reddish when young.

primaries: the main flight feathers at the end of a bird's wing which, in larger birds, can be seen as spread "fingers" when the bird is flying. Primary feathers normally number ten.

raptor: a bird of prey; one that hunts and kills other animals for food.

secondaries: the secondary flight feathers in a bird's wing, situated between the innermost primary feather and the bird's body. The number of secondary feathers varies.

still-hunt: watching for prey (usually on the ground) while perched.

scrub: brushwood or stunted bushes.

thicket: a number of shrubs or trees growing very close together.

thornveld: a bush habitat or woodland comprised of *Acacia*, *Albizia* or *Dichrostachys* trees, all of which are thorny.

understorey: refers to the lowest stratum in (usually) forest or woodland; secondary growth consisting of young trees, small bushes and annual plants.

valley bush: narrow belts of dense bush, often thorny and with succulent plant species, found in hot river valleys which drain into the Indian Ocean. Rainfall 500-900 mm per annum.

• REFERENCES •

Harrison, J.A., Allan, D.G., Underhill, L.G., Herremans, M., Tree, A.J., Parker, V. and Brown, C.J. (eds). 1997. *The Atlas of Southern African Birds. Volume 2: Passerines*. Johannesburg: BirdLife South Africa.

Irwin, M.P.S. 1981. *The Birds of Zimbabwe*. Zimbabwe: Quest Publishing.

Maclean, Gordon L. (ed.). 1985. *Roberts' Birds of Southern Africa*. Cape Town: John Voelcker Bird Book Fund.

Newman, Kenneth. 1998. *Newman's Birds of Southern Africa*. Halfway House: Southern Book Publishers.

Pooley, E. 1993. *The Complete Field Guide to Trees of Natal, Zululand and Transkei*. Durban: Natal Flora Publications Trust.

Sinclair, I., Hockey, P. and Tarboton, W. 1993. *Sasol Birds of Southern Africa*. Cape Town: Struik.

Urban, E.K., Hilary Fry, C. and Keith, S. (eds). 1992 & 1993. *The Birds of Africa. Volumes 4 and 5*. Orlando: Academic Press.

• INDEX TO SCIENTIFIC NAMES •

Page numbers refer to the page on which the
full species account appears.

Achaetops pycnopygius 82
Acrocephalus arundinaceus 70
   A. baeticatus 69
   A. gracilirostris 70
   A. palustris 56
   A. rufescens 74
   A. schoenobaenus 71
Amblyospiza albifrons 120
Ammomanes grayi 98
Anaplectes rubriceps 111
Andropadus importunus 87
   A. milanjensis 87
Anomalospiza imberbis 125
Anthoscopus caroli 44
   A. minutus 49
Anthus brachyurus 107
   A. caffer 103
   A. cinnamomeus 104
   A. crenatus 108
   A. hoeschi 106
   A. leucophrys 105
   A. lineiventris 103
   A. nyassae 104
   A. similis 107
   A. trivialis 103
   A. vaalensis 105
Apalis chirindensis 83
   A. flavida 59
   A. melanocephala 83
   A. ruddi 88
   A. thoracica 54
Bradypterus baboecala 72
   B. barratti 85
   B. sylvaticus 84
   B. victorini 76
Calamonastes fasciolatus 57
   C. stierlingi 46
Calandrella cinerea 96
Camaroptera brachyura 55
   C. brevicaudata 55
Cercomela familiaris 79
   C. schlegelii 80
   C. sinuata 79

   C. tractrac 80
Certhilauda albescens 100
   C. barlowi 100
   C. burra 99
   C. chuana 91
   C. curvirostris 94
   C. erythroclamys 100
Chersomanes albofasciata 97
Chloropeta natalensis 73
Cisticola aberrans 52
   C. aridula 65
   C. ayresii 66
   C. brachyptera 48
   C. brunnescens 67
   C. cantans 60
   C. chiniana 61
   C. erythrops 72
   C. fulvicapilla 44
   C. galactotes 74
   C. juncidis 64
   C. lais 75
   C. natalensis 64
   C. pipiens 74
   C. rufilata 60
   C. subruficapilla 75
   C. textrix 68
   C. tinniens 72
Emberiza impetuani 127
Eremalauda starki 98
Eremomela gregalis 81
   E. icteropygialis 52
   E. scotops 47
   E. usticollis 49
Eremopterix australis 97
   E. leucotis 92
   E. verticalis 97
Erythropygia coryphaeus 77
   E. leucophrys 56
   E. paena 59
   E. signata 86
Euplectes afer 122
   E. albonotatus 123
E. ardens 123
   E. axillaris 124

E. capensis 123
E. hordeaceus 125
E. macrourus 125
E. orix 121
E. progne 122
Euryptila subcinnamomea 81
Galerida magnirostris 94
Heliolais erythroptera 53
Hemimacronyx chloris 106
Heteromirafra ruddi 95
Hippolais icterina 49
    H. olivetorum 58
Hyliota australis 47
Indicator indicator 46
    I. meliphilus 86
    I. minor 46
    I. variegatus 86
Locustella fluviatilis 56
Luscinia luscinia 58
Malcorus pectoralis 82
Melaenornis infuscatus 78
Melaenornis mariquensis 53
Melaenornis pallidus 51
Melocichla mentalis 61
Mirafra africana 91
    M. africanoides 90
    M. apiata 93
    M. cheniana 95
    M. passerina 90
    M. rufocinnamomea 92
    M. sabota 90
Muscicapa adusta 50
    M. caerulescens 51
    M. striata 50
Myioparus plumbeus 45
Myrmecocichla formicivora 63
Oenanthe monticola 62
Oreophilais robertsi 85
Parisoma layardi 76
    P. subcaeruleum 57
Passer diffusus 115
    P. domesticus 128
    P. melanurus 116
    P. motitensis 118
Petronia superciliaris 116
Philetairus socius 118
Phragmacia substriata 81
Phyllastrephus debilis 84
    P. terrestris 87
Phylloscopus ruficapillus 85
    P. trochilus 43
Pinarocorys nigricans 92

Plocepasser mahali 115
Ploceus bicolor 84
    P. capensis 109
    P. cucullatus 111
    P. intermedius 111
    P. ocularis 109
    P. rubiginosus 119
    P. subaureus 120
    P. velatus 109
    P. xanthops 120
    P. xanthopterus 121
Prinia flavicans 62
    P. hypoxantha 62
    P. maculosa 80
    P. subflava 60
Prodotiscus regulus 45
    P. zambesiae 45
Pseudochloroptila symonsi 127
    P. totta 126
Quelea erythrops 124
    Q. quelea 112
Saxicola torquata 63
Schoenicola brevirostris 73
Serinus albogularis 127
    S. atrogularis 116
    S. gularis 117
    S. leucopterus 126
Sphenoeacus afer 77
Spizocorys conirostris 95
    S. fringillaris 96
    S. sclateri 98
Sporopipes squamifrons 118
Sylvia borin 55
    S. communis 58
Sylvietta rufescens 52
    S. whytii 47
Vidua chalybeata 114
    V. codringtoni 115
    V. funerea 114
    V. macroura 121
    V. obtusa 113
    V. paradisaea 113
    V. purpurascens 114
    V. regia 117

• Index to English Names •

Page numbers refer to the page on which the full species account appears.

Apalis, Bar-throated 54
   Black-headed 83
   Chirinda 83
   Rudd's 88
   Yellow-breasted 59
Bishop, Fire-crowned 125
   Golden 122
   Red 121
Bulbul, Slender 84
   Sombre 87
   Stripe-cheeked 87
   Terrestrial 87
Bunting, Lark-like 127
Canary, Black-throated 116
   Protea 126
   Streaky-headed 117
   White-throated 127
Chat, Ant-eating 63
   Familiar 79
   Karoo 80
   Mountain 62
   Sickle-winged 79
   Tractrac 80
Cisticola, Ayres' 66
   Black-backed 74
   Chirping 74
   Cloud 68
   Croaking 64
   Desert 65
   Fan-tailed 64

   Grey-backed 75
   Lazy 52
   Levaillant's 72
   Pale-crowned 67
   Rattling 61
   Red-faced 72
   Short-winged 48
   Singing 60
   Tinkling 60
   Wailing 75
Crombec, Long-billed 52
   Red-faced 47
Eremomela, Burnt-necked 49
   Green-capped 47
   Karoo 81
   Yellow-bellied 52
Finch, Cuckoo 125
Finch, Scaly-feathered 118
Finchlark, Black-eared 97
   Chestnut-backed 92
   Grey-backed 97
Flycatcher, Blue-grey 51
   Chat 78
   Dusky 50
   Fan-tailed 45
   Marico 53
   Pallid 51
   Spotted 50
Grassbird 77
Honeyguide, Eastern 86

Index to English names

Greater 46
Lesser 46
Scaly-throated 86
Sharp-billed 45
Slender-billed 45
Hyliota, Mashona 47
Lark, Barlow's 100
Botha's 96
Clapper 93
Dune 100
Dusky 92
Fawn-coloured 90
Flappet 92
Gray's 98
Karoo 100
Long-billed 94
Melodious 95
Monotonous 90
Pink-billed 95
Red 99
Red-capped 96
Rudd's 95
Rufous-naped 91
Sabota 90
Sclater's 98
Short-clawed 91
Spike-heeled 97
Stark's 98
Thick-billed 94
Neddicky 44
Nightingale, Thrush 58
Pipit, Buffy 105
Bushveld 103
Grassveld 104
Long-billed 107

Mountain 106
Plain-backed 105
Rock 108
Short-tailed 107
Striped 103
Tree 103
Wood 104
Yellow-breasted 106
Prinia, Black-chested 62
Karoo 80
Saffron 62
Tawny-flanked 60
Quelea, Red-billed 112
Red-headed 124
Robin, Brown 86
Kalahari 59
Karoo 77
Scrub, White-browed 56
Rockrunner 82
Siskin, Cape 126
Drakensberg 127
Sparrow, Cape 116
Great 118
Grey-headed, Southern 115
House 128
Yellow-throated 116
Sparrow-weaver, White-browed 115
Stonechat 63
Tit, Penduline, Cape 49
Penduline, Grey 44
Titbabbler 57
Layard's 76
Warbler, Barratt's 85
Barred 57

Barred, Stierling's 46
Bleating, Green-backed 55
Bleating, Grey-backed 55
Brier 85
Broad-tailed 73
Cinnamon-breasted 81
Garden 55
Icterine 49
Knysna 84
Marsh, African 69
Marsh, European 56
Moustached 61
Namaqua 81
Olive-tree 58
Red-winged 53
Reed, Cape 70
Reed, Great 70
River 56
Rufous-eared 82
Sedge, African 72
Sedge, European 71
Swamp, Greater 74
Victorin's 76
Willow 43
Yellow 73
Yellow-throated 85

Weaver, Brown-throated 121

Cape 109
Chestnut 119
Forest 84
Golden 120
Masked 109
Masked, Lesser 111
Red-headed 111
Sociable 118
Spectacled 109
Spotted-backed 111
Thick-billed 120
Yellow 120

Whitethroat 58

Whydah, Paradise 113
   Paradise, Broad-tailed 113
   Pin-tailed 121
   Shaft-tailed 117

Widow Finch, Black 114
   Green 115
   Purple 114
   Steel-blue 114

Widow, Long-tailed 122
   Red-collared 123
   Red-shouldered 124
   White-winged 123
   Yellow-backed 125
   Yellow-rumped 123